CØØØ137942

ARE YOU READY?

Stephanie's works have been specifically channelled to help you work through karma and what's occurring now – to propel you forward, to help you grow and recognise your highest strengths, gifts, attributes and personal talents – to help you to enjoy the life you live...

Internationally known and respected Stephanie J. King – Soulpreneur™ - works with the 'I am I' consciousness and the higher realms to reawaken each soul to its reason for being... to channel guidance, inspiration, enlightenment, encouragement, self-empowerment, confidence, understanding, love and healing – that's powerful, necessary, up-to-the-minute and applicable to all...

Again, are you ready to explore this?

"How can I explain the work of Stephanie J. King – except brilliant. Everything she does – she does with spirit. Every word she speaks – is channelled too. For many years she has dedicated her life to unlocking the potential of others, young and old, rich or poor. She works for the highest realms to empower and spur people on – to work on their own soul agenda, to access the talents, gifts and strengths they possess, to stir latent potential for the good of their own life and purpose, and for the greater good of the greater whole – the realms of Earth and Heaven as they combine.

"Every soul alive has karma to work through. Stephanie will not only help you recognise and work through it – but she'll elevate your state of consciousness for the remainder of the time that you are here.

"Her latest book *Grave Doubts* works on the same principles - only now ask a question - any question - and the answer will immediately be presented, like with a direct line - a telephone link - to what you need to know or work through now - this very moment. Nothing is beyond your ability to achieve. Stephanie J. King will unlock your potential and zest for living – whatever your soul purpose and presenting path..."

Jacky Newcomb,
Multi-award winning, Sunday Times best selling
author of An Angel by my Side

AUTHOR'S NOTE

This work is a three-way link between yourself, your angels / guardian and God.

Any reference to 'man' in this book is the universal word for humanity, for mankind as a whole. It is not intended to place the male gender over or above the female. All are equal.

All writing by 'I AM I' is channelled directly from God – from the Universal/ Earth/ Mind energy source. All speak directly with you.

For more information,
visit www.stephaniejking.com

SIMON

SYNOPSIS AND INTRODUCTION

(I am I). Life means birth and death but not always in equal measure. Every life existence must know both. (I am I).

How we live and choose to spend our time between these points is individually up to us. Many suppose a good life culminates in floating off to a better place, with the opposite being true when we've been bad. But who and what then sets that bar? What's determined as a good life? What happens to individuals who fit somewhere in between, who don't believe in Hell or Heaven or about what's coming later – and so are unsure? What if you've never pondered the real existence of the soul or questioned why you're here or how and why your life's unfolded as it has? What if you've been too scared or too wrapped up in daily living to take a look? What if, perhaps, you don't like what you see?

That's what happened to me. I was what you'd call a 'man's man', far too busy being real to even start to entertain such stuff and nonsense. I knew what I had lived through. No god, spirit, saint or angel, known or unknown, had ever shown themselves or spoken out to me. Nothing came my way without prior cost or effort; in fact the opposite was more my personal truth. Life had been a constant struggle, but also a game of choice and dare that I'd participated in to the max to raise my standing. From youth to adulthood and right up to this latest point, no one else looked out for me but my own self. So just imagine my annoyance when early one morning my wife woke me up and stated: "There was more to life itself and that I'd missed it – something so enormous, both exciting and mind blowing all at once." And she was right. I was actually blown away, alright – or to put this more precisely – I was livid! But then how was a fully grounded man, just an ordinary individual, supposed to react to that?

For anyone to suggest that I'd missed out on something big was more an insult, even madness: I missed out nothing – ever! I was streetwise, of sound mind with more than average common sense. In my view, I'd reached the top league of my game. Wasn't what we had and what we'd been through proof enough of it? Hadn't I shared everything? I'd given my level best. How was I supposed to react, to entertain such a turnaround of outlook and behaviour of someone I thought I knew inside and out? When someone you know that well announces from out of nowhere that they have healing powers, it was frightening and ridiculous both together...was she ill? In a matter of just moments (although from here now, looking back, life wasn't perfect) what I thought I had, what I had built and was about – was under question. I felt challenged – even cheated. My own internal being went into sudden turmoil and shouted NO!

That was just the start of what became a struggle, a wedge between us. I held strongly to beliefs that what I knew was correct and real. Nothing would change my mind. Hadn't I lived through every stage myself? Didn't I know the lows and highs I'd conquered and overcome? If I was wrong – what did it matter? If God was real, then *He* would know I'd done my best. If I was to be judged harshly – then screw that – once again, I'd done my best.

The here and now is what I knew. It wasn't great but I had tackled it head-on in my own way. I didn't want, need or believe in anything more. I was far too busy living, surviving, planning for the future, worrying about the present and what would happen if or when old age set in... What had religion ever wrought but war and pain, even within my own life: in-fighting between countries, people putting people against each other, beliefs against beliefs... NO. You could stick your higher thoughts. *I would be me.*

But then I *died*. Unexpectedly. In the middle of the night. Before my wife could even reach the bedroom light-switch – I was gone.

But little did I know...

I stood there, seeing my body limp and lifeless, bedlam all around me as my family panicked, went into shock, called the police and the ambulance service (by dialling 999) and then a friend and neighbour for more help. I watched the entire scene in its unfolding. I was dead – but still alive. Was this a nightmare?

Every effort was made to save me – but I was gone. My body couldn't cope with that much damage...

Grave Doubts is based on my personal journey from that point – going forward. It's intended as living proof that life continues after death, with knowledge of how and why. It's important that we know that what we go through here is not for nothing, that all remains with us as gains or earthly baggage, still to move through, carry – or to let go of if complete.

Each lifetime ends for all – this much is certain – but what comes next? Very few come back to tell, *but I must – because I can.* It will help me to advance in ways not yet available to my progression...

Regardless of who you are and the peaks that you might reach, very little in life prepares you for your death. And even less explains the deeper truths about life's meaning. What is life about? What's the point of being here, of all the hard work, sadness, stress and struggle – when in the end you go back empty handed and as naked as the day when you first birthed... What actually happens next? Why are we having this discussion?

If life just snuffs out, if there's nothing after that, then you'll be none the wiser in any case. But what if this information is correct? Can you risk such stakes? What if everything you've been and lived through contained a purpose, prize, another goal – if there really is a detailed, more serious knock-on side-effect that you'll carry forward further for lifetimes longer – if it's not correctly accessed, dealt with here and put to bed?

These questions shouldn't be left to our present half-hearted approach, to 'woo-woo' theories or to society's more general acceptance of the 'let's wait and see' or 'have faith and hope' mindsets deeply held by many.

My name is Simon. I had just turned 54 when suddenly I died in the middle of the night – without warning. This book is my own way of addressing what I sincerely thought up to then. I had shouted from the rooftops that such ideas were pure rubbish, false, unnecessary – because they challenged my own core beliefs, not just affecting me but everyone.

Nothing I had been taught had prepared me for my death (not that I'd planned it consciously), or even more importantly, had made any real sense of my life. But truths I now see make *this life, this time frame being lived* even more important to your progression than you could know; unless somehow you're really lucky and you do...

I want to give to life, to my friends and family, something back. I want the lifetime that I've spent to count for more, not because I must do this, but because I choose to and I can.

Please don't be like me. I was too stubborn, to the point of nearly missing what's important. Without this opportunity to now be able to write this book, I would have placed my journey's next stage in great jeopardy. To put things even more plainly, I would have needed to come back, to re-birth very quickly, to remember, realise and repeat much of the same content again – to then access different answers and live growth. Do you really want to repeat or go through all of that? I knew I didn't...

Life has a real-time purpose. It's eternal and unending. This means that you existed before your present birth and will be very much alive beyond your death. All that you encounter has more meaning. Put your thoughts aside for just a little while. Ponder this information and make up your mind yourself, but don't simply dismiss it until you've checked.

We do not die – we go on living! Yes, our body falls away, but we don't disappear, we continue from the same place we left off – with more besides. There is no shutting down – only change, transition, transformation and soul growth!

> *(I am I). Every time you birth you are supposed to grow, not only in ways physical, but deeper – at soul level. Every person living is here for specific reasons. It's important to understand this – to not miss it. (I am I).*

Simon

For more information,
visit www.stephaniejking.com

GRAVE

DOUBTS

DEATH WAS NEVER THE END

STEPHANIE J. KING
SOULPRENEUR™

Published by
Filament Publishing Ltd
16, Croydon Road, Waddon, Croydon,
Surrey, CR0 4PA, United Kingdom
Telephone +44 (0)20 8688 2598
Fax +44 (0)20 7183 7186
info@filamentpublishing.com
www.filamentpublishing.com

The right of Stephanie J. King to be identified as the author of this work has been asserted by her in accordance with the Designs and Copyright Act 1988.

ISBN 978-1-913192-13-6

Printed by IngramSpark

DEDICATION

To my family and friends – if anyone could do
this – you knew I would!

A REAL MAN'S AFTER LIFE STORY

Every person has the right to be happy in whatever way they personally choose. To be happy looks different to everyone. Not all will find it no matter how they try – but I did. I really did...

Life and people are not always as we would expect. Everyone wants to live as well as they can but not all fulfil all of their wishes. Not all get to tick all of their boxes. When you work hard, you get your reward; when you live a good life and become a good person again you receive your reward. But then again – do you? Even good people become down or sad. When you work your whole life to build up a life but people extract and expect more and more – it's easy to ask – what about you? What about the happy ending you've laboured to achieve? Where is it? When is being enough good enough?

I was a good man, a big personality: intelligent, no fool, a hard-working hard-playing 'man's man'. There was nothing I hadn't tried or explored to the max. I travelled, partied, loved, played and wrung every drop out of life that I possibly could – yet where am I now? At the age of 54, I died in the middle of the night, suddenly and completely without warning.

I had just been in bed fast asleep, nothing unusual there about that. Then I was dreaming. I was falling and falling in my dream. I landed but couldn't get my breath. I was in pain… I was calling, screaming for help, but the words were not getting out. My tongue was too large in my mouth. Somebody! Please! Help me! I woke up with a start – but the whole thing was real – the pain in my chest – I could not get my breath, was trying to shout but could not move my mouth. Pain ripped through my chest as I was trying to breathe or sit up or lay down unsuccessfully, my whole body an uncontrollable spasm. Every part of my self was immobilised. I felt weird, as though in a vacuum, being tugged out of myself through a wide open void that I saw was my body. Then I was outside, completely alive, standing next to myself still lying contorted in bed.

All mayhem broke loose around me as my wife ran to hit the light-switch and straight back to help. But of course it was no good – I was dead. But I was also still standing – I was actually still alive and still there watching everything. I saw everyone I loved trying every which way to revive me, trying to get me to move, to come around... This couldn't be real. I was going to wake up and find this was a terrible nightmare... but I couldn't get back into myself. I couldn't make words find their sound. I was still in the room – but unable to let anyone know.

They took me to hospital in an ambulance. My family went also in separate transportation, but despite efforts made I could not be revived. I'd suffered a huge explosion inside my chest. Hypertensive heart disease they called it, brought on by long-term high blood pressure and stress.

I was officially pronounced dead – but clearly I was still alive. I could see, hear, move and knew all that was happening. I was walking and calling – but nobody knew. What the heck was I going through?

Everyone was crying, everyone. I had to get home, to get myself back together, but in the next moment, already I was there. I was physically home without having driven or travelled myself.

What was wrong with this picture? What would happen next?

Nothing at all happened next. I was with my family all day. No flashing lights, no tunnel of darkness or light. Nothing. I was worried. What was meant to happen? I felt alive, completely alive without pain. I was exactly the same me as I always was, feeling probably a lot better than I had felt for days, yet I was supposed to be dead, gone, finished, snuffed out. And no one could hear anything I said!

Then it happened. Every fibre of my being felt warm as I was literally overwhelmed by pure love... Without hunger or time, in that moment what I felt was incredible...

I had never believed in life after death – yet here I was, completely fine and alive – but without 'a body' that anyone could see.

I worked out for myself how to enter and leave my own home, to be able to see those that loved me...Everyone I visited was in shock. Nothing was normal. Nothing was real. What on earth was I going to do? Shouldn't something have forewarned or prepared me?

CHAPTER 1

Whatever you imagine about death is far from the truth of reality. I had slipped out of my body so easily that in fact I was dazed, confused... even shocked...

I was as alive as I always had felt – whilst in front of me – I lay dead on the bed. Panic was the first thing. Panic everywhere, with everyone. I thought it was a mistake, that at any moment I would whizz back into myself and come around, dazed but alive, the way they depict on TV. But for me it just didn't happen. I needed to get help for myself.

I opened my mouth to shout out that I was still there and alright, but no one could hear. Though I saw people working to bring me around, I thought it would all be a dream – that I'd somehow wake up still safe in my bed, having just had the worst ever nightmare of my life.

While my body convulsed with the shocks they were giving me, I stood completely outside of myself. Every effort was made to revive me, but my body was damaged and it could not comply. When the doctors finally stated that I was dead, I stood beside my wife and my children in the room.

Nothing much prepares you first-hand for this experience. First came denial and shock. Then thoughts of what I would do. From life to afterlife in the blink of an eye. It's a lot to take in, to realise that you still exist, that you still feel the same as you did just before, that everything but nothing has changed.

Why? is what springs to mind next – why? What will happen to my family? What will happen to me? Thoughts raced across my mind in droves. How can you answer what you don't understand while witnessing your own death scene still unfolding? What next?

I was able to move around freely once I worked out 'how to control' what I could. Every time someone popped into my mind, I was immediately at their home, standing with them. It was a hard thing to witness their grief. Even those I believed didn't care very much were broken and torn by the news of my death. I was humbled and surprised all at once and was able to feel their feelings in those moments as if they were actually my own. Again no one and nothing can prepare you for the purity and depth of this experience.

I had no impression of time. I was trying to get someone to see me, to let them know I was actually there and OK. Even those I thought might be more ready and able to do this could not; they were stuck in their own sadness and pain.

I had no pain of my own. I felt free and incredibly alright despite the trauma of having just lost my life – or let's say my physical body. I can't say I was dead – because clearly I wasn't. I was perfectly well and alive.

I had never been one for religion. Every imaginable reason had turned me away from the church with thoughts of Heaven and any light, after-life realms. Had I been a good man? I think I was – as well as my character and behaviours had allowed me to comfortably behave. I didn't believe in a God watching over me – because too much had happened to prove that this could not exist.

Either I was dreaming the worst possible nightmare or I was still really clearly alive.

I began to remember what I'd heard that death and the first moments following would be like, but I hadn't experienced anything of that kind. I'd simply detached from my body. No amount of trying to change that would work.

Either I was insane or I would need to work out what to do, where to go now, how to handle what was happening or what I was supposed to do next. No one could see or hear me without feeling the searing pain of my loss. I tried to let them know I was standing there with them, that I was OK, without pain, surprised, even shocked, but OK. I tried to comfort my children and wife, but even they were too locked in their grief to take notice. At one point I managed to blend with my son as I stood directly behind him in his space, almost inside his shoes. I told my wife that it wasn't her fault, that we knew one day this would come – albeit not now, this soon, but that it would all be OK. These words my son spoke from his own mouth as my wife stood before him face-to-face with his hands holding onto her shoulders. She heard me! She recognised these words not as her son's but as mine. Thank goodness I'd managed to connect.

As fast as this happened, it was over. Even my son was surprised at what had just happened. He said he'd felt calm, a bit weird, and that the words he'd just spoken tumbled out...

Time was moving for me at a different rate than it was for all others around. To me it was fast, as though my death had only just happened. But for my family and friends, it was longer. Two days already had passed.

Everyone expects bright light and tunnels, but these did not happen for me. And where was the rest of my family – those who had died before me? Where was anyone?

For years I'd loosely thought that nothing beyond life existed, that at death we simply snuffed out. I decided that if I was wrong, and there was indeed a God presence, that I would be OK as I'd been a good man, not a saint but a man who had tried clearly to do his best. I began to think back through recent days and weeks to see if there'd been signals this was coming – but to all intents and purposes there were none. Admittedly I hadn't felt great for a while, but I'd never have guessed this would happen.

Everyone was broken up at the news. You don't realise how much people care, because in real life you don't always feel what you share. Stuff gets in the way – worries, stress, feelings, health and life. Thoughts, perceptions, suppositions, emotions can spiral way, way off the mark.

Think... think... what was I now going to do?

My family will find me if they too are alive. I thought. Dad was the first person who came into my mind as he'd only been gone a short while, just 18 months earlier. What about my mum and my gran? If they were alive, perhaps I could somehow reach them, but how? I saw no one except those I'd just left.

For a while I just wandered around. I was alive. I felt exactly the same. I didn't even hover or float. What was going on? Would I remain just like this? Was this all there was? Was this even all there should be? What the f**k?

Two days and two nights... I didn't sleep because I didn't feel tired. I didn't need food now, or drink. I was walking around and did whatever I wanted, but nothing made anymore sense.

During my life, I had clawed up through the ranks of whatever in life came my way. I'd been through the mill in more ways than most and had come out on top of my game. Was that it? Was life really a game? Did anything matter? Should it have been different – did I miss something, or do something I shouldn't? I was trying hard to work things through in my head. Was this Hell or Heaven? Was I stuck? Because the event was completely unexpected – did anyone know I was here? And where was everyone else? Where was this tunnel or bright light or something – anything? Where should I go?

CHAPTER 2

For years my life had been comfortable. I was not rich but had earned more than many. I'd paid taxes on time and also had a pension... I'd lived a good life with modern gadgets and holidays. My cars were pristine. I'd had jet skis and motorbikes, boats and motorhomes for enjoyment. Whatever I'd wanted I'd bought in a flash because I liked keeping up with technology. Although not rich, I definitely had more than most as reward for hard work and for doing things properly (well almost!). Yet inside I was never complete...

From a very young age, my life had been unsure and difficult. I won't go deep into personal business, but while fostered into care I was moved from place to place without notice, never knowing at bedtime if I'd be woken up early to be moved on once again before school. Care homes were every bit as you imagine them to be in the 1960s and 70s, and definitely not fit places to grow up in.

When finally able to stand alone and look after myself, I promised myself a good life, or at least a secure one. And this I had actually managed. No one banged on my door for money that was owed because all bills were paid as they landed. I was comfortably secure in my own home.

For the most part I was happy. Life was good. Yet inside, something always was amiss. I thought it was more along the lines of life being different than how I had always imagined. Responsibility and self-discipline that had kept me together were high on my list of importance. I made sure I did everything right (meaning 'properly') and on cue because somehow I felt that I should. I'd helped other people as well along the way, because when their chips were down I saw echoes of myself, of difficulties through time that I had faced. No one had been there for me and I knew how that felt, so I was wired to be ready to help. It allowed me to feel good and quite proud that I'd built up my life to be someone to be relied on, to be able to help as and when needed. From friends to acquaintances and strangers, I'd often helped all.

It gave pleasure to me to be this person. What was the point of all I'd been through if I couldn't then do what I wanted? But at some point, things started to change...

Every day became same-y. What I used to enjoy wasn't pleasurable anymore. Much around me became more like work, even pressure. I was living my life as I always had, but instead of feeling joy, I was stressed. Even my family was pulling me down – not really, but at least in my head. I was feeling the weight of the life I had built and now it was something I carried.

From outside it appeared that I had everything I wanted. But inside I felt sad and alone. Where was the life I thought I was building and the happy ever after I felt owed?

Now I could see my life and my story from a different perspective, as if looking at myself from outside-in. Still only two days had passed. I felt weird – maybe worried... Nothing was the way that it should be, the same as it was every morning. But then why would it be? *I was dead!*

My story was over, finished! But should it be? Had I died early? What could I have done differently to change this?

My son, wife and daughter were broken; even friends and people that I didn't know knew me were in shock. Yet I was shocked too!

In life, I was stubborn. I would not believe in life after death even though lots of proof was around me. Intelligent, I had a good mind. Analytical, even scientific, I had a great deal of knowledge stored within. I was sharp and missed nothing. I filed facts away until they became needed or until more could be added to make sense or to build up a picture. I had learned to control life, to make it work better for me. Having been through the mill and the hard stuff – I knew only to rely on myself.

So what now?

I tried to make sense of what happened. For the whole of my life I'd pushed hard at all boundaries. I hadn't thought of old age or of long term repercussions; I'd lived and played hard every moment. Either that or be bored or boring – but that wouldn't have really been me.

No, I had paid a high price. Everything I thought was important didn't matter in quite the same way. And not a bit of it made any difference to where I was now.

What was important I'd just left behind, my children, my wife and my friends. Everything else I could be without.

Thoughts and feelings raced... Where was my Mum? Why was I alone? Was there something I should do – or not miss? I'd never placed much value in wondering about any afterlife. My concern had been always with this life – what was next needed, wanted, useful or fun, how I would spend my next day. Occasionally I'd had daydreams/ thoughts of what I would like to do next, what would I like to be good at, what mark would I leave, what did I stand for. I wanted to break into new ground; I wanted to create some kind of legacy, for my life, my brain, my existence to mean something, to have mattered. I'd always admired those heroes who had somehow been talented or brave, who had put themselves out to add more to society and life. I felt ordinary and not talented or useful.

What I never really thought about, though, what I had never really wrapped my head around until now, was that in order to do that, in order to be remembered, in order to leave something significant behind you – you had first to leave. I had never really pondered that concept, that thought... I was so busy using up time, anyway that I chose, even allowing precious hours to go unused. I had never imagined a life beyond this one... Yet here I was, *still alive*. I would have to figure it out in the same way I'd had to figure out life – on my own. The point is – I'm alive, I am still alive. Something *will* happen next. I'm here – so I'll figure it out.

I had to get more of a grip, to understand my present situation...

First I tried to let my family and friends know I was there – but that didn't really work. A few times I was close but I couldn't get beyond their deep sadness. I felt unsure of what I really should do. In my mind, I just wanted to find someone who could help me here now. I just put my efforts into the little understanding I had. Why didn't I get the light or the tunnel? I was trying to find what I could/ should do next when I was suddenly then standing in my friend's house. He was crying. I wanted to help him, apart from his sadness, by letting him know I was with him...

Everyone knew I was a practical joker. I looked around to see if I could make a big bang. No sound would come. Eventually the door itself closed – but slowly. He noticed. Now I walked next to him. He felt me, but wasn't too sure. Nothing more, but at least he calmed down.

Every so often you wonder if life is the start and end of existence, if there is/could be more and if it has purpose beyond what we know now and live. But any feelings of what rational thought believes and produces are strong. We are taught about living, survival and struggle – but not about a reality that exists after death or about the impact/ consequences that this has on our actions through life. These things are left more to faith and belief, which to an ordinary person like myself was not helpful. I had to know something was true before I ever could accept it as truth. Silly I know. I had to feel and have physical proof...

My mother had been a good person. She was religious but where had that belief/trust gotten her? She was plagued with bad health and had operations that went wrong in the early 1970s, so never fully recovered. She prayed to God and to angels, but still she was ill. I wouldn't have been the same in her shoes if ever that had happened to me.

Because of mother's illness, my brother and I were fostered out. Dad couldn't look after two boys. We both went into care, into places that actually didn't care. We were just two more children to add to the numbers there already. I became tough. I was the brains and my brother the fist. Together we made sure no one bullied us. Eventually I stood up against bullies who bullied other kids, taking it upon myself to teach them all lessons in the only ways they understood; I bullied them into stopping. I was their warning to quit.

From then on, I became very streetwise. I won't share all the details of my life with you here, but you can already work out the gist. Nothing and no one would hurt me or my brother. I made sure. I was seen as a handful. My dad took my brother home but I was left in care. This strengthened my resolve to fight back. I wasn't bad – only I didn't take any crap. Why should I? Most things expected were pointless. My mind was sharp. Why should I respond to people that clearly didn't care or understand me? Let's not even start to mention respect...

I got moved around homes very often so didn't make any friends; I grew more and more independent and learned to rely on no one...

In a nutshell, I learned to rely on myself. The rest of my life was lived in that vein. Nothing would shock or surprise me. I built up a good life and on many occasions had more than my share of bad luck and heartache, which because I was strong, I bounced back from.

Everyone has ups and downs. I built up myself and my life to withstand them. Self-discipline was very strong. I felt it was good to keep myself and my life in good order to keep as much as possible as it should be.

But even this could not help me now. My life was over. Nothing more could be done. I was alive here and now, but my body was gone. Nothing I had done or had carefully put into place could help me understand what was going on for me here. Nothing, no matter how wisely planned, would come with me to where I was going. What had all of my struggles been for?

I was always a strong, stubborn person. If I couldn't see the point in something, unless I found proof or reason otherwise, I would not change my way of thinking. I knew I was intelligent. Nothing could get past me. I was good at working things out and very little would make me give up. I was never a quitter, and so too I wouldn't quit now.

I was as alive as I always had been. There had to be something I was missing. If I was alive, then so probably were my mother and father – but where? I went to my father's old house, but of course he wasn't there. We'd buried him a year and a half ago, but it was at least a place to start looking. I went to Kent to the church where we'd placed his ashes, but again found nothing and no one. I went to visit friends, mainly because I could – to pass time. Life was going on as you would expect after the shock of my passing.

I wished for my mum to come and get me. She was the one person I had always missed the most. If I was alive, then so was she too. Now I just wished I could find her.

Time had no meaning. I went where I wanted. For me it was nothing more than a little while – but for family and friends – days came and went and still I could not get to grips with what was happening.

CHAPTER 3

It's said that we all have a book somewhere within us. It's a shame I had to die to write mine...

My wife has written some books on the importance of soul. I thought it rubbish and so refused even to try to understand it. A complete waste of time... It made me mad that she gave so much to it.

Was this the reason I was alone now? I had given her a pretty hard time. She tried to tell me there was much more to life but I didn't want to listen or know. I would find out when I died if that was true – but before then, my focus was on living. The whole topic had made my blood boil, but then wasn't that why I was where I am now? Too much stress, too much hard living... had I enjoyed the drink a bit too much? I used to also enjoy recreationals... This I believed I could definitely control – but my body had just proven otherwise.

I was here, but no longer in body. All around me was the same as it was during life – only now, I myself had checked out.

My heart had exploded from high blood pressure. Well the main arteries had, anyway, so it amounts to the same thing. Earlier in the year I'd had what the doctors supposed was a mini stroke. My symptoms came and went. They said I may never get another and that sometimes these things happened for no reason without prior warning.

To backtrack a bit – I was under the doctor for high blood pressure. Being a stubborn man, I took the tablets but didn't really do any more than that. I felt invincible. Self-discipline meant I could always carry on regardless. I pushed and made myself work that way because I was still proving to the world that I wasn't a wimp. Nothing would ever hold me back. I would never and had never let anyone down. I'd made sure of that. But had I now let myself down in the worst possible way through being too stubborn?

When I'd had my mini stroke, the doctors MRI'd my neck and head because my symptoms were tunnelled vision with zig-zag colours and lights coming in. They lasted for a matter of half an hour or so, and then subsided. My wife made me visit the doctor to get it checked out. My scans were OK. I wasn't worried. Stress was an issue because of work – I had my own business – but other than that all was OK.

Regular check-ups at the doctors were made periodically, but I wasn't always truthful. If I'd had a few drinks or had partied the night before, I would make an excuse to cancel the session and rearrange it as I knew my blood pressure would be affected. I didn't want the doctor to judge me – so I only went when I knew my test readings would be OK. I never thought anymore about it than that. Didn't imagine this would be a problem.

My wife had wondered why they didn't MRI my heart when I'd had my supposed mini stroke, but because I was stubborn and would have definitely kicked off, she didn't say anything. In hindsight, if my heart had been checked they would indeed have found a problem manifesting!

But how would you know you are wrong if you really don't know? I thought I had everything under control. If I knew that my body was running out of credit – I might have then made better choices. Sure I wasn't kicking fit, but I had more miles clocked up on my two mountain bikes then I'd travelled for years in my car and motorbike put together, just from short but regular daily rides in all kinds of weather, even frost, rain and snow – really just because I was stubborn. I was still proving to myself that I still had some old fight within me...

(I am I). Everyone is afraid of death but we know that it will come to affect us. Birth is actually more painful than dying. But how many people really look at their journey to see what it looks like from another perspective? How many can be that objective?

Remember that the body itself is only temporary. It's there to allow you physical life and physical movement in a physical world. Nothing more... It does need to be taken care of because you need it to last for as long as it can in the best possible condition. Again, nothing more...

Some try to stay super-fit to maintain it. This is good, as long as you then use it wisely for your journey and purpose. But at some stage, body dies anyway. Sometimes this can happen seemingly out of sync with expectations and plans. What then is left? When the body falls away – what is left?

The soul is what's left. That part of you that thinks before you even get chance to think, that knows or intuits before you do. What have you done to learn more or understand about that?

When physical life is over – soul gravitates back to the level it came from. If you're lucky you will have done well and will have grown, you'll have changed your vibration to enable you then to move forward. But not everyone does. Many have done no work in this area at all. That's why they come back – to try again in physical reality to grow. (I am I).

I was alive. I decided I would only accept that I was now termed as *dead* if I could see or find my own mother. She was a good person. I was a good person. If I am alive, then perhaps so was she. I wanted living proof again. I wanted her to come for me as the movies had depicted. I could wait. What else was there for me to do?

Everything felt peaceful. I had no pain. I wasn't thirsty or hungry. I felt good. I couldn't remember the last time that I had.

Eventually I found that I could go wherever I thought I would like to be – so I went to see everyone I knew. I felt I was saying my goodbyes as I didn't know how long I would be around and still able to move in this manner. I had no notion of time. I went to everyone I knew and to those who knew me – if only very little. Some felt my presence, so knew I'd been there, but mostly they were sad over me...

Nothing would make them feel better. I became weary of trying to make my presence felt. I guess I became more accepting. Still, I hadn't seen another single soul living as I now did. Where were all the people who had passed much like me – before me?

Now I felt very emotional. It's sad to leave those you have loved, cared for and known for so long behind. I knew I couldn't be like this always. But for now I was at least comforted by the knowledge that this was a phase I'd pass through. Don't ask me how I knew that – I just knew.

Behind me was my life. How I now saw it was different than when I was in it. Now I could see what I had – how lucky I had been in so many ways that while I was in it, I'd overlooked. I didn't take things for granted, but I just didn't see the whole story.

Because of my upbringing, I had learned to be strong. I had built up a good life and a good social standing. I was respected, admired, looked up to by some. Whatever I wanted or needed I had without waiting or wanting. You could say I was in my abundance, but I never really saw it as that. I was busy building and planning for the future my pensions would bring. Of course, the downward financial spiral of the promise of those pensions affected me. Hopes were getting smaller as the pensions became less and less than intended. Still I worked and paid into them hoping always for the best to occur. I wasn't rich, but I was doing OK. Now I was gone. The stresses I'd had were gone too.

Now all that mattered was my family. Nothing more. Friends and family are the real prizes of life. All you build up – in any direction – is gone at the moment of death. Everything vanishes. It's you and you alone standing there.

I remembered times I had worked hard to build up my career, my house, cars, toys and social standing. What had I done those things for really? How much had I spent? I had enjoyed them at the time and I'd shared also with others, but this had only made me want even more. So I had more. Had I been mean? Not outwardly. I had shared. But really I had lived for myself. Yes, I always made sure those around me were happy and cared for, but I never really looked outside of that box.

The world I was part of was all I could handle. Worldwide affairs I saw but gave no more attention to, because in truth they then made me depressed. I didn't like what I saw or where things were heading. I was charitable and kind where I could be – but again thought no more about wider life than that. I'd left all the hard stuff behind me. This was my own time to build a good solid life – so I did.

But inside, was I happy? Not really. I was always searching or reaching for something that I could never find and couldn't name. I thought I'd found it in many ways previously, but soon the old pull came back to want more. Now what had I gained? All was out of my reach. Nothing mattered because in my present state, I was gone. Yet I was alive and still feeling and thinking. I was the same me, the same person. I could see myself clearly and I looked still the same – but I was no longer part of the scene I was seeing. Nothing left and nothing more to gain. So what had I lived all this for? For what reason had I had my life? Why had I worked, built myself up, stressed and struggled, to then stand here alone as I now am... Things were not really making good sense.

> *(I am I). Every life lived is a gift. It's a journey of discovery, of survival, expression, exploration and creativity. Nothing is impossible. All options are open without bias to every soul. The routes travelled and chosen are individual. Personal choice, free will and the unwritten, uncreated laws of discernment and attraction are the tools. (I am I).*

Everyone I had known who knew and loved me was in pain from the shock of my passing. My pain was in seeing this and not being able to make them feel better. I had no way of letting them know I was there. No way to say "I'm OK". No way to make peace or to tie up loose ends still unfinished.

Why was I living? I was dead, but so clearly I wasn't. My body was lifeless but I was the same as before.

My thoughts, memories, knowledge and knowing were all still intact. Everything I knew before I still knew, and now even things I'd forgotten. I remembered in detail every aspect of my life. I had time on my hands to think through it.

No one had prepared me for this. I did not go to church because I wasn't religious. I was more often angry with God for the hardships I'd lived through and witnessed – so why would *I* go to a church? Vicars and churches were corrupt in my opinion, preaching what wasn't real about a God who provides for us all. I had provided for me and my family. Not God. Where was this God when I was in pain? When my mother was ill, when my tiny 10 day old baby had died, when all of the bad stuff in youth and when older occurred? Where was God when children were hurt or murdered, when Auschwitz was happening, when bad things all over the world are still happening to innocent people? NO. God and religion were not there for me – I was sure.

(I am I). Nothing bad in the world ever stems from Myself. All happens because of input from human actions, of thought, intent and behaviour. I am unable to override anything, for to do so would negate the gifts of free will and choice. This of course cannot happen. So life has no choice but to play out and finish what's first put in motion by people. (I am I).

Much of my worry and stress had stemmed really from me. I know that now. I was a worrier. Not outwardly, but certainly inside. I was the cause. Life happens. Stuff happens. What is key is the way we choose to handle or take it on board. I was determined to keep a tight hold on everything. Nothing would get one over on me. I had been down to the lowest point I could get to. 'Never again' was my vow. Vows to self are very powerful mantras. We often forget we have made them as life shifts and moves forward, but they remain with us as programming we've set that we then have to work with, sometimes long after the time those words were thought or stated.

I was getting better at moving about. I went everywhere to see everyone. Nothing was the way it ought to be. Was I to be like this for always? Why was nothing working as it should?

I had time on my hands. I was never really good in my own company – so this wasn't a great predicament for me to be in. Where was I going? What was I meant to do next? No one was here to help. What if my life had not been good enough? I didn't expect to be alive after death. I didn't even expect death... Yet here I was, caught in the middle of who knows what with nowhere to go and nothing to do except what I myself wanted. Was this hell? Was it Heaven? Was I to remain here until the natural time came that my body should have passed? I'd died earlier than expected – so was this limbo? I racked my thoughts for knowledge of the afterlife, but very little appeared. I only knew what I'd seen in movies, had heard here and there or maybe read, which now when I needed it turned out to be little. I'd put all my efforts into living, into being alive. *Yet I was still alive!* So what next?

People round me had dabbled in what's now termed as the 'esoteric' at different stages of my early adolescence. To be honest it had scared me. I remember walking into a room where I didn't realise a group was still sitting with a ouija board, when a glass shot off the table at incredible speed and smashed. WTF?? At other times, I'd glimpsed shadow people I didn't know in my own home or in my shower and they'd always made me jump. They vanished just as quickly, but I didn't want my knowledge to go further. I'd heard of hauntings and of ghosts and I didn't want to know any part of it.

My choice was just to live. I chose life. If there was an afterlife, I would find out when I died. If Heaven and Hell did exist, I'd decided that Heaven would be too boring anyway, if it was anything like going to church. I hated churches. The smell, the hymns, the 'holier than thou' approach of priests – who behind the scenes molested children and were every bit as bad as the rest of the world outside – even worse in my opinion – as they presented themselves as humble and good. No. Heaven was not for me but I didn't want to burn in Hell's eternal fires either. Apart from that though, it did seem a more fun option with parties and such like...

I guess the fear of Hell sitting in the back of my mind had kept me on a better road in my life. I wasn't a saint and didn't want to be. I was a 'man's man'. Took risks. Did stuff I sometimes really shouldn't have, but at least it made me feel alive. I never hurt anyone deliberately, I put others before myself – but I pushed all the boundaries I could. My body had paid the price on more than a few occasions, but I was strong, resilient, well built. I handled all that came and won through it. I guess coming through things became my victory. I showed others, and especially myself, just how far I could go. No one could stop me. 'No' was to me my red flag. I found ways to do and be almost everything.

Now how far had it gotten me? My body was gone. It was broken. I was here with nowhere to go, nothing to do and no one else anywhere around. Why? This was starting to bother me. If I was good, God – if he existed – would know. If I hadn't been good enough, that would be known also. So where was this tunnel or door? I was not able to help my family and friends anymore. But I also couldn't stay as I was. Where was my mum? I wanted her now. She was the one that I wanted to see to believe in life continuing. No one else would do. I wanted mum.

Ever since I was a little boy, I had taken care of myself. I also had to help mum when I came out of school because already she was ill way back then – from the effects of that big operation. Dad worked. I looked after my brother, myself and my mum. It was just something that needed to be done; my brother was too young – so I did it. That's how life was.

I was the head of the house very often, as leadership came easy. This had stood me in good stead throughout most of my life, really. Never afraid of a challenge, I faced life full on. Sometimes life or people sure got to me, but that's more personal stuff that doesn't really help the matter here. I guess I'm just saying I wasn't a wimp, nor was I afraid to step up. I could find a way out or over most things. But not now. Time was not behaving as it should. I was skipping huge chunks as I'd travelled to see friends and family, not venturing too far just in case I missed something I needed or really in case I missed some kind of opening – you know – like those portrayed in *Ghost* – the old Patrick Swayze movie.

From the perspective of where I was now, I was learning all kinds of things that either I'd missed or just hadn't been told while alive. Even my family carried information that for one reason or another they couldn't share. It's strange how we do that – I mean filter what we think is acceptable, or if it is not, we hold back. More often it's done out of love and respect, sometimes through fear – fear of what the consequences might be.

I thought I'd been different – more open than most, but now as I looked back, I saw that I too held things back or displayed what I wanted to be seen or known, not consciously, but because that's how life often operates. Everyone saw me as a big guy with a big heart. They thought I was tough, but they only saw and knew what I'd shown them. I was very sensitive, but that came out more often as jokes and having fun or as a side effect of the drink. I loved everyone, really I did, and I wanted to feel that love back – but in truth, I didn't often feel it returned, not because it wasn't there but because I didn't recognise love's language. I knew how to give out and that was that.

People were not the problem. It was me. But because I'd always set myself up as a helper – more often people came when they needed help. I gave and they went away. Every once in a while, this got heavy. Where was help when I needed the same? It wasn't so easy to come by.

Family was my root and my life, friends a close second and having fun next. Any aim that I had was to make my life easy and great.

Eventually, I'd visited everyone. Everyone was in a state of shock. No one could have guessed this would happen – and most certainly not to me.

Four nights had now passed and with the first morning sun came my mother. She looked younger and healthier than when I saw her last. She was happy. I took her hand and I flew into the light that had also appeared. It was as easy as stepping out from one room into the next. I felt her love. My own love responded. It felt perfect. I felt perfect. All other thoughts and ideas fell away. Nothing mattered. I was going to a place somehow I recognised already as my home.

Everything was bright and pristine. All my family members were waiting to see me. Dad had passed on just 18 months previously. He too looked a picture of health. I looked at everyone and each person was happy; no one seemed surprised at my arrival. It was natural. For the very first time I could ever remember, I felt the loving connection I'd searched a whole lifetime to find. Wounds of the past for now were all gone. This perfect moment I would not forget. I was home.

For a few days we rested and talked. I was shown around. It felt more like a holiday, a well-deserved break. Everything was beautiful – even perfect.

Every now and then I'd think of the past, of my family and the life I'd just left.

Early one morning I was told to get dressed because today was the day of my funeral. I was present throughout the whole thing. Again I was taken aback at the people who were there and the miles they had travelled. I felt their sadness and pain – but even more I could feel their love. I was loved...

Life is funny. It's possible to get so locked into your story that you miss half of what's really going on, even when you're smack-bang in the middle of it. From where I now was I could see layers and layers of feelings, emotions and thoughts swirling around every person. It was like shimmering light in a huge array of colours around everyone. Each person was light – but in different shades. It's surprising again just how much we miss with our own physical eyes – even given the complexity of how mind and eyes operate.

CHAPTER 4

Every part of my being, my senses, my emotions and my thoughts were alive and active. I was alive. My thoughts were quick, almost super-speed. My whole family too was alive. Nothing else mattered for the moment. Thoughts of death and the recent past vanished as I became caught up within this reunion. I saw friends I had lost horrifically over time. They looked the same as they had when they'd been alive, even better, younger, happier, healthier. They glowed with love for me. I was overwhelmed. On the side-lines stood more people I knew from work and life activities. They were all here as part of my welcome – a total surprise, extraordinary...

No one prepares you for this. Very little is said about life after death in this manner. Beliefs are held within certain circles, but the wider consensus is more focused on ghosts and ghostly noises, spooky stuff and the occult. No one expects the pure love that awaits us at homecoming. I have since learned that this welcome isn't the same for one and all, but for most who have done their best. Heaven (just a label) is vast (I am told). Many ways of return reflect different cultures, needs, karma and beliefs.

I had not been an angel, was always a handful by anyone's standards, but I had done the best that I could. Everyone has baggage. Everyone makes mistakes. That's how we learn to be better. But in truth, I had tried to live a good life without trying to become something I wasn't. I was streetwise. My upbringing and life had been difficult. No one had been there to molly-coddle or fuss so I'd had to control my own path. Fairness was important. Even to the point of getting myself into trouble for standing up for myself and for others. I was strong, I was big, with a good heart and mind, and I used it.

Ever since I'd lost mum during youth, I knew the real value of life. I wanted to use every part of it. Nothing would be out of my reach. I had to be free. I did what I wanted and pushed all I could to the limit.

Everyone I'd thought lost for good was around me, even people I had only briefly met but had had dealings with. Even those I hadn't really been kind to. No malice was here – just acceptance and the pleasure of welcome.

Each person welcomed me personally with acknowledgement of what had then occurred. We didn't talk, but somehow conversation occurred through inner knowing, thoughts and strong feelings. It was an equivalent to reliving the moment. No malice – only understanding and truth. I saw myself from their perspective as well as my own. Many things were suddenly obvious in ways not understood by me before. I felt their love and their pain. I saw the effect of my smallest actions and words. Every action and response, small or large, was being acknowledged.

Eventually the greeting was over. Time had no hold; it was as if there was no time. All was just as it presented.

How did I feel? I was open in heart and mind. Surprised and aware in ways I didn't know possible. I had only just arrived and already my world was wide open and making more sense. I could see the value, the vulnerability, the fear, love and pain that for years I had carried and thought tightly under control. I saw how these things had *controlled* me; how they were always behind all I did… I understood more about myself and my life in that moment than

I'd understood throughout the whole time I'd lived.

I was taken away then for some rest.

Before death, I had not been religious. I wasn't an atheist but I just wouldn't conform to the church. I'd seen too much hardship and pain. I didn't believe in God because in my own world – if God did exist – then he was more cruel... How can such things occur to innocent children and people... How could he be saying on one hand 'I love you, I'm there' – and on the other 'I'll smite you if you don't conform to my bidding?' The two conflicting versions didn't tally...

I tried to live a good life within the parameters of things that came up. I wasn't a saint – far from it – but underneath, I'd tried to be just. If God did exist, then he would know me for the truth of myself. Sure, I'd have to face up to my actions, but in line with what had occurred. Heaven was not on my radar as I didn't want floaty and boring. I'd always had excitement and fun. I would hopefully find more of the same if life did continue, I'd thought, or maybe I just would snuff out, but in that case I wouldn't know anyway.

Yet here I was. A million miles away from what I'd expected or wondered.

From where I was now, life looked the same as life I'd just left. I could walk and interact. I could feel and know who I am. I was still me. I still looked the same. I didn't float and didn't pass through any objects. I was as solid as I had been before. Here, life still looked like Earth. I was thinking and feeling intently. My recent life itself was a whole world away, but I was the same. I touched and I felt and I ate.

Where was I? I was in a building much like an apartment. Everything usual seemed present except television, telephones, white goods... Electrical equipment no longer was necessary... The sound of footsteps approaching pulled me out of my thoughts. My guide had arrived to speak with me.

Nothing happened. We just talked. Layers of understanding had to be sieved through. Apparently I was lucky that I got here so quickly. Most people are not so received. I didn't need to go through to rehabilitation. I needed understanding, explanation and rest. Much of life had taken its toll on my energy which needed to come back to where it should be. Natural concerns about my family and the life I'd just left were overwhelming. I was told that I could visit and return as much as I wanted, but first I should try to rest.

For the first time in a long time I was given peace of mind, for now I was not in control. With nothing to do and nothing more to be done, I had to simply let go and just rest. For me this was alien. I'd always taken worldly life and used time to its limit – but here time rules didn't apply.

Thoughts came and went. What mattered most was my family. I'd left life rather swiftly, but while there I'd almost planned for this moment. I'd done all I could to provide for what they would need. I'd really done it for myself towards my old age and retirement, but in the event of my death, natural transfers automatically kicked in. Now I could do nothing else.

I was told to rest but I couldn't. What was going to happen next? What about retribution – Heaven or Hell? This hadn't been discussed. Nothing had really, except concerns about life left behind and the fact that I was still here after death – alive, talking, thinking and being.

Sunrise and sunset still occurred (but I've been told that's not the same everywhere, with some places having perpetual light). My surroundings, though unfamiliar, were the most beautiful I'd ever seen. They instilled a sense of stillness and peace – the way that standing by the ocean did on Earth... I say on Earth because that refers back to my old life. Here it still very much seemed like the same Earth. No sci-fi scenery or colours. No masters or aliens in sight. All was serene and very lovely. I was alone. No one came or went. I could walk, sit or rest – the choice was my own. Worlds apart from where I'd just left yet really just the same – I was alive and still much my old self.

CHAPTER 5

Anyone who knew me personally knew how much I disliked my own company. I needed people. I loved people, interaction and fun. Being alone too long with my thoughts used to result in the negative, so I'd invent things to be and to do. Here it was different. I found peace. I was alone, but at home in life's beauty. Everything was calm. With no agenda and no place to go, I was in a place of suspension.

Alone with my thoughts, I looked back.

If someone had told me much earlier that life categorically continues, I would have perhaps used it differently. My wife tried over many years to say this exact thing but I didn't believe or even want to listen. How could she – a person I'd known for so long – wake up suddenly one morning and have all the answers to life? It was absurd, even comical. How could she be right? I was an intelligent man. Not highly educated, but I had taught my brain to retain general knowledge, facts and wider information. You could even say that my mind was almost photographic. I could take random information, unconnected in the moment to specifics, and file it away – to bring it back in perfect recall later on – to make sense of or to add more to life still unfolding. Not being greatly academic, this was a talent I'd perfected to retain and use knowledge. I missed nothing. I thought I knew quite a lot. So how could I have missed something so significant as that which my wife told me I did? I thought she was ill. Worse still this knowledge was changing her and our relationship. Far away from acceptance – I hated it.

We learn from youth that life is there for us to use, explore and to enjoy. That we should exercise intelligence, strength and power to harness it, to gain a good standing, quality of life, happiness, wealth, wellbeing, a good name and personal power. We learn to read people and events to fit in and feel we belong. We work hard and grow into what we'll become. Not necessarily into what we'd like to be – but often based on what's available and the choices we make, we become who we are at any moment. I thought I'd had a good handle on this. In fact, given my upbringing and circumstances unfolding, I'd thought I'd done pretty well: I'd given, I'd shared, I'd been kind – not an angel – and yes, I did have a temper and faults, but I'd given my best. Now suddenly I was being told by my wife that all this was not enough, that I was not seeing life's truest picture, that a whole other level existed... It was too much to swallow – to compute for a person who was on top of his game...

Instead of being open to the possibility that this could be correct, to investigate and to find out myself, I clammed shut. I just wouldn't go there, wouldn't even entertain the idea. I hated religion. It was a bane in my life. I wouldn't hear that this wasn't the case.

Now it was time for my guide to collect me. I was allowed to venture further afield. My only contact so far had been my initial homecoming. Now I was ready to see more. If you're wondering what life looks like here – for me it looked very much the same – only cleaner, brighter, more fulfilling as scenery around was taken in. I was able to rest and even sleep. I still ate and drank, but hunger and thirst were not as prominent as when I was alive. I ate because that's what we do. I drank because I thought I was thirsty and thought that really I should. Conditioning within us runs deep.

Travel was not mentioned. I had to shut my eyes and go with it. I didn't fly or float – we just arrived. Words are not adequate here to describe this experience. I wasn't allowed to go anywhere alone yet as apparently I was still being helped.

The next few days and weeks were spent as personal to me, to my rehabilitation and personal story. I was going to be OK. Nothing to report – only that I was at peace. No malice or condemnation crossed my path. Love/acceptance were unconditional. It's hard to explain with limiting words – but it's like being accepted completely, like being cocooned so no harm or hurt can get in – except there was no harm or hurt anywhere. I could examine all parts of my life and my journey without the pain I'd experienced previously. Not in a disconnected, uncaring fashion, but completely engaged and alert to feelings and emotions and the wider understanding they represented that I hadn't known or noticed before.

My thoughts were less about self – but more of my attachment and understanding of life. I could see how I'd created my story through ideas, thoughts, perceptions, choices, decisions, discussions, assumptions... I saw how I'd taken information and had used it to then shape and create my existence. Some of it good – some not great... I'd put a lot of emphasis on wanting to be accepted, loved and happy and had wanted to prove my success. I'd put effort into building and retaining to the point it had taken control. I'd succumbed to the pattern of many – in that I had taken care of current physical needs and surroundings – but had not contemplated or thought deeper about soul.

My happiness had been outwardly projected as something I had to make happen or find. I had actually found plenty – but it came and then went just as fast. That meant I was always wanting more. I found it in activities, in family, friends and what I did as a result as I built, lived and managed my life – but then because it was based on those things, when conditions changed so did my own view of life and happiness. Nothing hit the spot or made me feel whole or complete for very long. Life was up and it was down, but I had learned well to juggle and to keep it up there.

Now from where I was I could see the pressures I had placed on myself as well as on those who I loved and cared for. I had turned love and friendship into a full time job instead of being able to just be and flow with what occurred.

We don't always realise the demands we put on self or others along the course of normal living and relationships because we're driven by thoughts subconsciously. We believe what we believe, want and think, expect what we expect and that is that. Who we feel we are, what we look or yearn for becomes normality. Life is the way it is and that's all there is to it. But then it's not that... We just don't look any deeper because we don't even know that we should. We just accept our experiences as truth and fact.

When you tell yourself that something's real, you then believe it is. When others tell you too, it then becomes often rock solid. What solidifies stays with you as part of who you are to form beliefs and character that define you.

My beliefs I had thought wide and open, but now in retrospect I saw that I was Earth-bound, believing more in science and information than in the esoteric. Science fiction was my limit. Ghosts and more I'd come across, but to me it was not something in which I'd wanted to dabble. It had never sparked a fuse to look further – but the horror and consequences I believed in. That was the totality of my understanding. I was unprepared to investigate further and never attached it to a continuation of actual life...

Everyone has limits. I know mine – or I did. But in all matters physical I'd been prepared to push the boundaries until I had none. So why was I completely the opposite regarding this stuff? I couldn't answer. I couldn't explain...

From an early age I'd been grilled in right and wrong. Everyone has rules, I'd broken more than most, but inside I always knew I was good.

Misunderstood – completely... abandoned and alone – yes, that was me. I was the hero of my story – for no one else really knew the true inner me, even those who I thought really should. I was unique. I was alone. I would be strong and show the world what I was made of.

CHAPTER 6

Who was in charge of me? No one. Who would tell me what I could or couldn't do? No one. Who took care of and looked after me? No one. I was responsible, dependable and there for one and all in times of need – because I knew just how it felt to have no one else to turn to, to be alone against the hard knocks of life.

In truth, I was a rescuer although I didn't know this. I blazed a trail that others could choose to travel or perhaps not. I was good at life and living and so I shared this.

Now how much of all that was still here with me?

I can say I'd lived a relatively good life, I'd taken it to its limit and done my best. I'd provided for my family – not always without protest – but we'd enjoyed the finer things. Bills were paid on time. I owed nothing to anyone. But had I felt complete and happy? I'm not sure. As before, I was able to see pockets of feeling whole... but these came and went like weather has its cycles, times of light and dark – so that's how I now saw my life.

Everything had had its place. Nearly all had left its mark. I could see it was my own attachment that had decided how and why. I had allowed my own subconscious to be the ruler over me instead of coming back to central peace and balance.

Nothing was the same now. I didn't have that internal pull. I could see, reflect, and dissect without the pull of fear, emotions, success or failure... I was unbiased. I was open. I was beginning to understand on whole new levels, levels I wouldn't access while in my body – not because I couldn't – but because I wouldn't. I'd been too stubborn.

> *(I am I). No person is ever alone. It's just perception that we are. In truth, all are joined. All work together or remain in opposition. How each life then pans out is freedom of choice, freedom of will. Once all options of search, trial and error have*

been exhausted, peace will always return.
(I am I).

Now, as if a huge fog was clearing, I saw life, my own especially, in ways I didn't really know existed. Like a hologram overlaps and each part is the same as the whole, I could see the life I'd just lived in the same way. I thought I had been different, singular, separate – but I was the same as many others. Personal sadness as well as triumphs were the same as other people's – only while we are in them, we don't realise we're enveloped.

I saw the many times I'd been too hard on myself and on other people, expecting way too much that would affect them then in other ways. When we're in the story we can't always clearly see it.

Even during childhood and later in adolescence, I could see from the perspectives of my family. Deep in pain and trauma and the hard times of the sixties and early seventies, life was not so easy and opinions not as open or forgiving as today. General life and understanding were quite different. Times were not as difficult as they had been during the war, but the country as a whole was still rebuilding.

Many children were caught up within the cruel world of the social services and what occurred behind closed doors to the vulnerable. It wasn't always the fault of the system which was built with good intentions, but of the people who ran or worked within it. I was one of those children caught up, so I vowed life would be different when I could run it.

Honesty and integrity were foremost for me, along with discipline and morals. Being disciplined with myself had brought me focus. I was not a saint – far from it – but I also couldn't stand cowards or bullies. I fought the bullies to give them back a taste of their own medicine. Coming from a background of 'stay tough or be broken' – I'd stayed tough. Once or twice I'd closed my eyes to things I might have changed, and these memories then stayed with me all my life. That's what drove me forward to become the man I was. Nothing special really – just myself...

There is purpose to my thinking from these perspectives now because I hadn't gone away or disappeared when I had died. Life continues. It doesn't stop. All we were, we take with us, not always as physical live conditions, behaviour or habits, but as knowing, as memories, understanding and past input...

This experience will be different for all – depending on what occurred during life. I was in reflection, understanding, healing and higher soul growth all at once. They called it rehabilitating and letting go of Earthly Baggage, to see what has been learnt and what is left. From here I would go on when the time was right to who knows what and how or where. For now I had peace and rest and time outside of time to reflect, to digest, to make sense...

My funeral came and went. I was there. I was surprised and moved by the love and sadness: love I hadn't really felt while still alive. I'd been locked inside myself from the inside looking out, because the hurt and pain of life meant I couldn't believe in truth and peace. I'd seen too much, had lived through too much that couldn't be discarded as insignificant.

Don't imagine for an instant that I was melancholy. In fact, I was the opposite. I was a practical joker, always playing, laughing, teasing other people. It made me happy to make them laugh, to push their buttons and their boundaries, their awareness... Always good at telling stories – I'd had plenty of them to share to delight my friends and family and even strangers. I was a 'people person'. But the trouble with being a joker is that no one then knows when you're being serious. I had loved life. Used and abused it as well as my body. No regrets for all I'd done – for I'd been lucky. There was nothing I wanted to do that I hadn't tried – well, except going to the moon. But I did have a tiny piece of foil that had come from a real live rocket in Houston, Texas that had been there – and now was mine (although ironically I'd now left that behind too!).

Fun was what I was known for. Fun and reliability... When anyone had a problem, they came to me.

That's how it was. I asked them to. I lived well and had more than I needed, not rich but comfortable month on month. But this then became a problem. I saw myself as being used. Maybe I was, maybe I wasn't, but instead of love coming forth from those I helped – I felt many only came to see me when I could help, bar a select few. I couldn't stop being me, but I wished they'd include me in their pastimes, their pleasure times, as I always had included them. I was lonely – even when I was surrounded by people.

From my current perspective, I can see that this loneliness was produced by me. I had been off balance emotionally which then computed physically into feelings and my personal actions. I was sorry for the pressures I'd placed onto those I had loved. I'd made them responsible for my happiness instead of working on me, myself. I was the fun guy that everyone liked to have around because I brought laughter and more to occasions. When in a crowd, I was happy. Alone, I was up and often down.

Each person has their own baggage, I know. I'm trying to highlight mine to help others see beyond stuff they're carrying – because it matters.

If life didn't continue, then the option would be just to get through the time we live life in the best way that each of us can, to be happy, to hurt no one and live well. But that's not the case. The truth is far more important. I'd died before I realised – and now I am writing this book – that's how important this is. Instead of going forward – I remain static. I am doing this to help where before I was stubborn and living a half-life without knowing the deeper consequences that would follow.

(I am I). Each person has an allotted time span within a body that will help them live a life of their own choosing whilst on Earth. This experience is temporary – but the results of that existence last forever – both for the soul concerned and for life's own evolving process and morphing picture. (I am I).

CHAPTER 7

What will looking a little deeper at life really cost? For me, I was stubborn and scared. This stuff is deep. I was good, really good, at finding flaws, working things out and highlighting untruths and errors. What if I were to find flaws in this? What would I do about that?

Beliefs such as these run parallel with life. Everyone carries them somewhere. Some play them out to the annoyance of others as endless examples of do-gooders – or to the other extreme – as 'poor me' types. Some believe in absolutely nothing, others in science alone. I was perhaps more in that camp. I loved knowledge and science helped me prove what was *real*. I wanted the real because that I could physically touch, see and hold. If I was honest I didn't like *airy fairy* rubbish... and belief without proof fell into that. I'd worked too long and hard against a cruel and hard life. If God did exist then he was no friend to me. I was good – but he was nowhere in sight. All I had, all I'd built, all I'd been through was down to myself, down to stress, hard work and survival. No God anywhere. But I'd always shown up – to help me.

What I had been through may not have been worse than many others had lived through before – but I was still carrying the scars and the memories of a lifetime. If I let those go, where would 'I' be? I was all I'd expressed, seen and witnessed – not some of it, not part of it, but the whole complete package. Pain and success gained were my trophies.

It's strange looking at life experiences with the blinkers taken off. You see your whole existence from a completely different angle – as though looking back in from outside, connected yet disconnected, and yet more truthful because you've nothing to lose, use or gain. No one needs to be right or to win. You just see your own life as it is – factually.

I was seeing my story and the interaction of everyone I'd met – strangers, family and friends – as if from the vision of life. I guess that's what they mean when they say that your life is reviewed. I'd had the flashes of memories as if on film while I was waiting for mum to arrive. But now I was receiving an overview... What I was getting was coming in from myself, so there was no one and nothing to argue or fight or deny or agree with. Only truths, understanding and acknowledgement...

Everything was OK. I was OK. I would be OK. Even though I didn't know where I was going or what would happen next, I just knew it would be alright.

Life is a strange mix of uncertainty, discovery, experience, expression and growth. We imagine it's a continuous line going forward. But we don't see the effect of our actions beyond the immediately physical. We live as if we all are sealed units – disconnected, alone and surviving for all of our worth. But from where I was now I could see a different picture emerging.

Life is more like a film that never ends. Each person has a role of their choosing that's made by their self, by the way they collect data and process it. No one is separate at all. Invisible feelings, fears, likes, dislikes, love, hate, scars and trophies produce energy, signals and cross-currents that we access, individually stamp and process. Just like a string of computers connect, we're more like life's own live computers, biologically creating as we live. We all connect with each other, even to people, places and things happening across the other side of the world. Why didn't I see that? As communication and satellite systems send signals across time and space – so did we. We were the working, gear-type, cog parts of life itself. Just as our cells communicate with one another to make our own body work, we each are the very same to the Earth.

We do not die – we go on living. Yes, our body falls – but we don't. We continue the same as where we left off (within reason). There is no shutting down or dispersing – only change.

We are creators – for the creator. We live, attract and manifest all that we personally seek, see and operate.

CHAPTER 8

During life I tried to mask what I was thinking and feeling by turning to things that temporarily seemed to make me feel better. Drink and recreational substances were my choice – not all the while – but at times I chose (and thought I deserved…). I thought they made life feel better. I was happy and carefree in the company of these things and my music, sometimes with others, but often alone. I felt alive and complete. I loved how I could hear and feel every note of the music. I called family and friends to say that I loved them. Boundaries, inhibitions, barriers fell away.

From an outside perspective, I had everything. But inside, my life was emptier. Living a good life was still not enough. Something was missing. I thought I had *lost my edge, gone soft*... I projected that onto my family and wife, thinking they were the cause, or that they didn't spend enough time at home with me – or even onto friends, insisting they came over more often. I was still looking outwardly for happiness and love that I believed were not present enough. I thought family should be more like the US TV programme about American family life, based on the life and trials of a 1930s and 1940s Virginia mountain family through financial depression and World War II, *The Waltons* (1971–1981). Although we ourselves were all strong and good – I felt I was missing some vital ingredient that in some way would make me feel whole.

I gave my best and expected love back in return. Really it was there all along, but from my perspective I just didn't see it. I was searching for something that looked different.

From where I was now, once again another picture was starting to emerge.

It's funny how life unfolds. From this higher, disconnected but intuitive connection, I could see more clearly what I'd had. They say you don't recognise what you've got until it's gone and in many ways that saying is true. What I'd had was far more than I'd realised.

From very early on, I had wanted stability. I could now see in retrospect that I'd had that. I had wanted independence and freedom from constraints. I'd had that also, with the biggest constraints by far having been placed on me by myself. Without knowing, I'd lived life from inside a box of what I thought life to be, of how I thought it should look and pan out. Even though I believed I was open – and in so many ways really I was – on deeper levels that drove the real me, I was still searching for the happiness I believed I deserved but didn't have.

Life gives us what we believe and expect – but I didn't know that. By chasing and wanting what I thought I was lacking – life was giving me the same in reflection. I didn't know I was creating what I least wanted – myself.

My wife had tried her best to help me see and wake up, but my highly intelligent mind would not let me understand or accept it. To be honest, I just didn't want to. I now know this to be a product of ego, an inbuilt part underpinning the self that's very strong. What she was saying was in many ways far too simple. I'd lived through the hard. We're programmed that life is hard – so when someone is in front of you saying that it's not and you are wrong – you don't always hear or want to listen.

Children, when young and innocent, have a way of cutting through life's 'crap' by saying open honest truths without prejudice. They can shock you into seeing what's obvious. Because of their innocence without deeper agenda, they make you think and can change your outlook and make you feel humble. When adults tell you things in the same way it can make you feel annoyed, even arrogant. Up come the shutters. You shout them down and walk off. Who do they think they are to give you advice? What a ******* cheek!

My wife was one of those people who could see beyond the apparent. She had a deep gift of insight and understanding that my worldly beliefs would not fathom. I thought she thought herself above me – I, who had given to friends and family – everything. I had been angry and had taken it wrongly.

Now that my life was over and it was too late to take it on board to make changes, I could see undeniably that she was right. I had missed probably the most important ingredient of life completely because it was too easy, too simple. We're programmed to believe life is hard – so we get hard. Fundamentally, life has to supply what we expect.

Things were making more sense...

Body is just the outer crust, the mind the inner layer. It's easy to be detached from the body – but more difficult to be detached from the mind because we feel it to be more our true self. If someone says that your body looks ill, you don't feel offended because you are not so attached – unless you live more for your body and how it looks. But if someone says your mind seems ill, disturbed, or that your beliefs and thoughts are in any way off course, you feel extremely offended. You feel that you've just been insulted. With the mind you are nearer to your real self. When someone says something offhand about your body you can tolerate it, but if anyone says something relating to your mind, to beliefs, it's less possible to tolerate that because you feel you're hurt deeper. They've hit deeper with their comments that hurt.

Yet mind and body are two separate layers that work and blend as one to make us whole. We don't separate the two ordinarily; we don't pigeonhole these aspects as working apart from one another. Because we don't realise the separation, we are driven by mind, by the thoughts, beliefs and feelings that we generate. Just as if you have a house, the whole thing is visible from outside – the outer walls and structure – and from inside, the internal walls and structure. The body represents the outer layer, while the mind is more like the internals. In this way, the mind is closer to you – but in fact it is still a body – more subtle, but a changeable cloak just the same.

In death, your body perishes but the inner 'mind' stays with you. We are so attached to our beliefs that even death cannot remove them easily from us. Mind continues – all memories, all core thoughts, beliefs and existences remain part of who we are until the time that we are able or ready to release them.

In life, I'd lived out my beliefs as absolute. In death, I could now see they were but passing phases that could have been explored, replaced and updated... In youth we learn and grow and move forward. But in adulthood, we often don't think that is necessary as we're all grown and we reap just rewards from hard work.

In youth I'd possessed very little that could be called my own. I'd vowed my adult life would be different – and it was. I'd had a good life that I'd built up by myself and I had not been prepared to think that I'd been blinkered; that even more exists to life on more levels...

CHAPTER 9

Either I was dreaming, still asleep in my bed, or this stuff was real, which I knew it was. I was alive – still am alive – minus my recent life lived and physical body. It's as though a film has ended that you were a part of. As though a story's finished and no more can be done to change a single part to refine or make it more or better. My life on Earth was physically over. I could not do any more to make it different. So what will happen now?

It was time for me to leave the house I'd been convalescing in. Because of my recent understandings, I was ready to move forward. This will be done in different ways for each of us when we are ready, depending on needs, requirements and understanding – just as it would be while still alive physically on Earth.

It's difficult to express in words what happens here. Just as thought is instant when you think of things – it's even quicker over here. We travelled almost instantly to the places I would be needing next. I tried to do it myself later on – but could not.

I put personal thoughts aside, for now I was to work, not for the sake of working but to learn, grow and help. I was not ill so I didn't need to rest. I fully understood where I was and what had happened to get me here, so I didn't need a doctor or a team of experts to get me back onto the road of wellness. Instead I now had to become a helper to help others...

Many of us feel better when we can be of service. This doesn't alter by being here – instead the need continues much increased. To be of service gives you aim and goals and purpose. Right now I needed purpose. I needed to be busy to stop wishing I was home. Now I was the student needing help – but at the same time giving help in the process, just as a baby instinctively helps another baby when it can... It's part of our intrinsic nature to reach out...

My surroundings were urban. We were in a place of rehabilitation. At first glance this seemed more like a high tech hospital, clean, clear, bright and bustling in appearance. This is where I would have entered into the realms of spirit ordinarily had I not needed my *aloneness experience* or been able to make the adjustment as well as I had. I was to help here for a while to also grant me more perspective on my current situation.

Much was as one would expect – rooms off rooms, waiting areas, people walking all around of different types – not aliens, just people. Doctors, nurses and assistants took care of many patients. I couldn't see or tell their ailments unless they'd been damaged by war or incident. Most had helpers with them just like me. I was surprised at the scenes I saw because to me it was all unexpected. Remember to all intents and purposes – I'd just died myself – yet here I was, surveying scenes I would otherwise have avoided whilst on Earth. I'd never liked hospitals (I'd known too many people who went in and never came out).

A buzzer sounded and I was ushered into a room just to the side. There had been an accident and someone had died. They were already there with us but they were screaming and disoriented. They had to be sedated to be calmed. Their arrival, to this person, was a shock. They couldn't grasp that they'd actually just died. Disoriented and confused, still believing they had pain, they were distraught. From real life – to life without the physical body – will be more than can be accepted if the person was really earthbound – as I also had been, the only difference being that now I had a basic understanding that more exists...

Since I came to be here, the only people I had met were those I knew and those who helped me. Now it was like being in the middle of the whole hospital. People were everywhere, but they all had purpose. No one paid any attention to me or to my guide. Instead we were left to take a look around.

Day and night had no meaning. What that meant was that the level of activity never ceased. Yet all was calm and welcoming despite what was clearly going on.

What was going on? Hundreds of people appeared to stay or to pass through here, of many nationalities and creeds. Their commonality was trauma. They were confused, frightened, angry and even injured. This being their first stop without their physical body, they had no knowledge of where they were or of what was happening and why. Everyone had someone with them as a helper. Many could understand once explanations had been given, usually those with previous religious knowledge, that the afterlife is real and they were in it. But others were too sick or angry to face this current stage. They required specialist help to work with needs presenting. It is a shock when you have died and you didn't see it coming – when you have died but are alive and more alert than you were even moments before. Not everyone believes in Hell or Heaven. Many come from violent deaths of war or homicide, deliberate or unexpected, not to mention accidents and illness – long or short.

Each soul was met with love and care and was given complete attention to match personal needs. Even though they had been injured and no longer had a physical body, their attachment to that body and the hurts they'd faced were fresh and real. They still felt the pain and trauma because they'd been killed. They could see they were alive and so had the emotions and the feelings that went with it. Everyone was taken to their own room. Many were sedated (not in ways you'd expect when in body – but by other means) to help them return to calm or to understand and then help them mend. You must remember that pain and trauma are energetically depleting. The act of dying or being killed is traumatic to say the least. Not all welcome this experience, *the experience of still being,* with open arms. I was lucky compared to these souls; I was helped and able to comprehend fairly quickly because of things my soul knew from before. These people needed more care, more patience, more time and understanding. They hadn't even met their family yet, because they weren't ready to greet that experience.

(I am I). This was a half-way house, a place of rehabilitation (one of many different

kinds within the vast network of these healing halls). First recuperation, then once souls can accept their current status and regain peace and balance, they can reunite with their families for support, further understanding and love. (I am I).

CHAPTER 10

I was reaching a point where what I was seeing was too much for me to handle. Remember I hadn't long passed over myself. I hadn't liked to see others in pain when I was alive. Their pain hurt me physically. I felt it. But seeing it here was overwhelming...

From morning till night the admissions were endless. I pushed my own feelings to one side and braved through. I was here to witness, to watch and learn from the experts... Not everyone was frightened. It seemed that when they had an understanding that life does continue, no matter how small, the transition was easier – if not always accepted, as no person really wants to leave their family and loved ones to move forward, but at least an understanding of the situation made it easier to accept that they were still alive after death.

I was told why I was witnessing these scenes.

To know that life doesn't simply snuff out is important. It means the consequences and leftovers of what occurs during this life in some form follows us into the next; the journey is ongoing. Everything is recorded within the records of soul. Nothing is missed, not only from the perspective of each individual themselves, but from wider angles playing out unseen and unnoticed – called karma, cause and effect.

Live contracts play out simultaneously while we're in body. Much occurs over and over again, like the movie *Groundhog Day*, until we realise and change it, not as punishment but as opportunities to do better, to make life better, to make better choices or to mend what at some point earlier broke down.

Every person has a limited time span to live through. It's just that through the process of birthing, we forget. We win or sometimes lose at different stages. In life, we believe we must win at all costs, but in truth it's life itself that supports us, only we ourselves have to steer it correctly...

If we knew categorically that life continues, that nothing is hidden or goes by unnoticed, we'd take better care of the journey; we'd realise consequences are real. Take now, for example: I was learning the need for even the most basic understanding that life doesn't actually snuff out. That when body and soul separate life still occurs as before...*life carries on.* I myself had carried on. I felt the same as I did before passing – only healthier. The truth is that when we are still in body, unless we look in a mirror to see the reflection momentarily, we don't think in terms of body all day. We just are. We feel, think, experience, express, explore and create from a place that emanates from inside. We just *are.* Body is really just our temporary casing, that's all. It's the thing, the vehicle that gets us around.

The need to understand this was not only important for life after life to help with transition, but for physical time lived as well. To know that your story continues, that what is not corrected, finished or is wrong will be worked through again next time round, perhaps not in exactly the same manner – but in variations of what's needed overall.

The story itself is never ending. You take it with you. And most importantly, everything matters, really *matters,* for wider reasons/repercussions of personal development and whether we go forward, remain static or choose to come back to repeat aspects of the same process over (not instantly but always by choice for soul reasons). I gave my best through the whole of my life, but found out too late about this stuff. I was a good person, but my soul hadn't gathered much more... but it needed more, to be able to gravitate to other levels that would allow me to gain much more growth. During life I didn't know I should feed it, not in terms of religion and repetition, but in terms of understanding my own personal life force and its connection to what for me had played out.

I was now learning first-hand what in life I would not accept. Nothing was forced. All was placed before me in ways I could now understand. From within I was finding life's answers to questions I hadn't even realised I had. (Some people now do this while still on Earth – it's called their awakening.)

Every person is equally treated because all souls are of equal importance. No one is left in unnecessary pain unless for some reason short term they still need it, to gain something from it, with the exception of children – being innocents.

Next I was introduced to a nun; once again, things were not all they seemed...

Each helper is really a more evolved being, who for reasons of service and personal calling or growth had elected to take on a charge. Usually their charge represented what they themselves had at some stage overcome and learned from. I was being looked after by the helper who would help me adjust and learn from my past/present experience.

For me, one of the thorns in my side had been religion. My mum had been religious; she prayed and believed in the greatness of God, but that in the end hadn't helped her. She still became sick and died much too young, thus leaving me and my brother as two little boys. I also wasn't happy because religion (in my own view) had altered my relationship with my wife. No God could really exist or the bad things of the world would not happen to good innocent people. So to meet a nun here was not what I expected or wanted to do, especially one who for now was assigned to assist me.

I had manners. I kept personal thoughts of liking or disliking to myself (although nothing here can be hidden – I didn't know this). I was to help her, to watch, learn and to try to assist. I pushed personal questions aside and got on with matters presenting.

Every person needed to be told where they were, to not worry about future or past, that this was just a place they had come to for now until they could accept and recover. The biggest shock for most was that they were living at all. Pain was assessed and their ability to understand what they now felt was memory-based, linked to their body and what had just happened. Disbelief for some turned into anger and rage at the current situation, at any involved in it, at the fact they had left loved ones, friends and things they thought were important – but more often at the fact they had no idea this would happen or that now they could do no more to adjust or amend their life story.

I understood what they felt because I had just come through the same thing myself, with the difference between them and me being that when I passed, I had already begun to question what I realised I was learning to be true. That life continues. That how we personally process live energy was the culprit of much that we feel stuck within. (When alive, I wouldn't even speak the word 'energy' – as it represented what my wife talked about. Even that simple word would make me see red with anger and rage.)

Every one passing through this place was traumatised because they were 'still' here. Only those with higher understanding were accepting, more available, prepared to listen and learn.

The nun was paired with me – or more correctly I with her – because of my aversion to the church and to the stories of my youth I had heard, seen or witnessed. Here was a person who had believed wholly in God. She had her own reasons for doing this work – but for now it was to help me wake up. I didn't think that after the experiences I'd just come through, I needed waking up any further – to still be myself, alive after physical death in every way as before and much more…

I tried to make myself busy and help.

Sedation was not drug-related here. Forms of energy emitted from rocks, and crystals and things that looked more like weights and talismans were used, each having their own particular property, vibration and unique energetic healing force.

Every person had a story they had gone through. Not all had wanted their life to be over but I was learning that many had had choices at some point that would have taken their life to different outcomes. I learnt also that this was not a place suicide or murder victims came to. They would need extra special treatment and help. This place was more for *intermediate* care after passings, such as my own. (Although many different afterlife entry points exist – depending on what occurred and what was next needed by each soul. Life has its own way of working this out.)

Before I had passed, in my times of being down I used to sometimes think that I no longer wanted or really enjoyed life. Events of the world pulled me down. I didn't like what people were doing to the planet – not from a do-gooder's perspective – but from the well-known naturalist David Attenborough's accounts, from the wars, famine and fighting I saw all around, from the simple freedoms of *The Waltons* and *The Darling Buds of May* (a popular British TV series, 1991 – 1993, which adapted the 1958 novel, set in rural Kent, following the life of the Larkin family) and how these innocent behaviours were becoming further removed from real life society. How the cost of living was becoming sky high, how every promise made by investments and pensions was failing and falling short... I had been disillusioned and tired of life, thinking it held little for me. Now I was here helping those who screamed for more time... It's ironic how life places us in situations that force what's opposite to stand out. I was wondering if my own life could have been able to have been more stretched out...

Every evening I went home – or back to the place that I called home for now at least. I was feeling more balanced and useful. Friends began to stop by. We talked and shared our experiences. Just like me, they too had had to understand and adjust. None of us had felt that we'd completed all we could have, but agreed that it would have been useful to have had this extra knowledge whilst still living physically, so we could each have made some adjustments here and there...

A new understanding was beginning to take shape for us all. Where we were was a half-way stage between what is understood to be 'Heaven' or the higher levels of love, peace, contentment and light – and the lower extremes, getting denser and darker by degrees. This place was allowing us to decide whether we wanted to go forward or return again to physical life at a time, place and level that would help us try again to grow forward. It wasn't necessary to make that choice now, but at some future point it would happen.

I learnt that many levels exist, that you gravitate towards the one closest to your own soul's vibration depending on the life you'd just led. That was why it took so long for my mum to appear when I'd first passed. She had been gone a long time; her energy was much finer than mine. The closer to Earth you exist the heavier and denser the energy vibration. The closest thing I could give in explanation to this is how it would be for us as we venture towards outer space, where the atmosphere becomes thinner and we then are less able to cope. It seems to work in reverse when we're souls without body any longer. Bodies need gravity. Souls don't. Gravity is heavy for a soul, much like being clothed in lead all over. The pressure is heavy, immense.

Because I was working in the way I now was – I was growing. Everyday presented something new. Even now (some years later) I still look back at that time with gratitude for what it helped me to see and understand.

Each live event, whether here or when physical, has something within it to teach us – something to give or to share. I could see we were joined energetically, that life is a subtle dance of give and take. No one can win and no one can lose because we all are live active parts of the same thing. Growing up never happens. We just change and evolve as we go along – except that not enough people do. Everyone feels their own life and truth most important – but again, this is not always correct. We all form part of the same segment in time, the same live storyline playing out. Everything connects to affect and to change something else. Even people who fall out, who for years haven't spoken, affect one another by thoughts and feelings they carry directly. They keep the feud going with live energy they're each feeding to it whilst at the same time still blaming one another.

The events of real life were more intricate, but easy and more visible than anything I had ever imagined. That's why it's stated that a child will enter Heaven much more easily and faster than any adult, because they're naturally open and innocent until further agendas kick in. They carry less baggage, no expectations, no preconceptions; they live in the real moment unfolding as time runs along.

That's why I had refused to acknowledge what my wife was writing about. I couldn't believe something so important was that simple.

I was getting the picture.

Physical life and what for now we can call *the afterlife* were not really very different – from this current level at least – and remember what you will experience may differ in varying degrees, as things differ from person to person, city to city, country to country on Earth...

(I am I). Now you can see the importance of understanding your personal connection to life in terms of soul and soul growth. Rebirth and ascension are not mystical legends for some far off point in evolution or existence. They are happening all around every day to all people, whether living physically or energetically in spirit. No one is immune from this happening. All have birthed physically and all will at some stage move forward. How easy the transition, whether physical or spiritual, is uniquely up to each individual concerned. (I am I).

CHAPTER 11

I know everyone wants to know information relating to what the afterlife looks like – but as stated already, for me it wasn't really much different to look at. Colours were brighter, crisper, cleaner with more hues than on Earth than you can imagine. Night follows day follows night in the usual fashion, only time is not measured in precisely the same manner. References to days, morning, noon, evening and night are more often used.

Because transportation here is rather more instant, when it's time to meet someone they simply show up. It's born more from a place of inner knowing than about thinking and measuring time. Everything happens at the right time. If resistance occurs in any measure, then the timing isn't quite right. Synchronicity works in the same way in life when different aspects of what's needed converge or occur simultaneously as if right on cue.

There is no litter, no graffiti. This probably exists in the denser lower levels but not here. And remember – this place is intermediate. It's possible to remain here for a very short while or considerably longer – like years, decades and even centuries. We'll talk more about that a bit later. Remember that people gravitate to the place most in tune with their energy (initially at least), as dictated by actions and the life that's been lived. All things thought, done, achieved or unfinished while living on Earth translate back into your energy signature. In other words what you produce/do/overcome becomes your vibration – your visible shading of dark or light. In a realm of pure energy, your soul energy being visible is how you're then seen from that point, as in how you'll present or appear.

To understand this further, you need to know about auras and chakras, and about energy centres, but we don't need to go into that here. Many books have already been written on the subject, including within my wife's channelled works.

Before passing I believed my beliefs, all I'd lived through or learned or thought truth. But that knowledge is limited. It's barely the tip of the iceberg.

What is the real purpose of living? I myself had asked that same question often – but didn't really find a good answer. Life is a struggle – whether you are rich or poor, educated or not – it's easy to get stuck or caught up, and the only differences are in the ways personal things become processed. Worries are still worries. Needs are still needs. None of these make you complete. That's why regardless of whether you're wealthy or not, you still search for what you feel to be missing. Hundreds of labels are placed on this search as we try to secure what is lacking. More of this, more of that, less of something other... and so daily the search continues to drive and control us in ways we don't always realise.

But how often do we say: 'that's enough. No more searching...'? And even when we do – we simply swap one storyline for another. At life's end, as you take a look back, you can see that much was illusion. Often people are playing at life – but many simply don't know it. But often again what we believe is real life is merely just a stab at existence, of what we *think* life and living should look like or be about.

As old as you are – are you happy? And how long does that happiness last? Do you feel whole and complete? Are you valued and recognised for your efforts? Do you win? Has life panned itself out the way you expected? Are you happy with what you see around you?

No one can be happy all of the time, but when you can live in reality with your eyes open, totally balanced and largely content for the most part – then believe me, you're doing it right. Few even get to reach that place...

Everything here did look similar to Earth at first glance but with huge subtle differences...

No rubbish or pollution. No electrical goods as there's no need for such. Things needed are instantly available with nothing unrequired produced. There's no waste or abuse of any kind. Not because we are all saints and angels, but because only what's required is created. When something becomes obsolete or no longer necessary – what was – reverts back to pure energy.

At every given opportunity I worked to help at the hospital, not because I was made to, but because it helped me find purpose – for now at least. It was good to be making a difference. No rewards were given because there was nothing I needed myself. All my own needs were met. On Earth I had very few. If we're honest and we strip our own personal life back – most people could really say the same. We just get caught in the trap, the loop of the journey and also the commitments we're living.

I was placed in this hospital so I could see the value of the work my own wife was producing. She wakes people up to their own gifts and strengths, to the recognition they're of value and part of something bigger. When alive I'd poo-pooed this as poppycock, but here I was learning the need, not only so that when someone passes they know that their life will continue, but more to the point – so they can start to get happy, to feel loved and necessary, to grow and to fully live, integrate and appreciate the value of this one!

A lifetime is more than the time spent on Earth. The fact I'm still here – writing this book, channelling through my own wife – is true proof. The question of why should also be asked. That life continues – you are learning. But why is it so important to me to relay this to you? Why do loved ones, family and friends come forward so readily through psychics and mediums? Why aren't we all off on a jolly? We don't have to communicate our presence and unfailing love – but we do... Not only to say we are part of your lives still, that we know what you're doing and what's going on... It's to prove that life really continues. We don't fall asleep and wait for some future miraculous awakening when God comes to sit on the throne – to discuss what has passed. We're all living and alive even now. No one is left lying in a hole in the ground in their grave. That's just their shed earthly remains...

You fall asleep every night. Your body doesn't move anywhere. Yet you are awake and aware on other altered levels. You go off exploring and have many adventures as real and as powerful as any live experience or reality that you live. *Part of you never sleeps.* It doesn't need sleep, it doesn't need rest or food – for those things are for the benefit of body. We label it dreaming – but only because we are told that it is. Someone a long time ago put that label there, so now that's what we call it and then we dismiss it. The same thing is true when we're awake and living life. A continuous dialogue occurs always in the background that we've labelled as chatter of the mind, as just our internal thoughts; we also travel off in the day wherever we wish and this is accepted or termed as day-dreaming. But it's the same thing. No difference except one occurs during sleep and the other whilst alert and awake – and it's precisely this part of us that continues.

So again, why am I writing this book? Why do loved ones try to prove they are close, that they're OK and really safe?

It's not just to prove we're around, but to prove that life really continues.

But again, what does the significance of that statement mean really?

It means that what you are or have been continues the journey along with you. That what's achieved, done or left undone goes with you too as part of your continuing story. This is a huge deal. It matters to every soul in existence. Earth is the place to overcome things, to put them to bed and move forward...

We've been looking at life as a product from start to finish between birth and death, with death being the final bumper – the end. But that is not true – there's much more.

We've had physical lifetimes before. At the end of each one, we go back to where I am now because our body has gone, we can't continue physically on – but we don't poof away, we don't snuff out or disappear. Instead we gravitate – like steam or gas without the dense mass of our current form – to wherever our soul finds its best fit. (The same thing occurs in Earthly life. If an ordinary person was removed from their family and story and plopped into a country estate or a rocket ship about to take off – they just would not fit; not because they couldn't do so, but because at that time they'd be little prepared. Without the practice or know-how to handle it, they'd be completely out of their league/comfort zone/energetic vibration – whichever way you would care to look at it.) Once a lifetime is over on Earth there's nothing more that can be done until next time (with exceptions we can speak of later). So each soul naturally gravitates/transcends to the place it has earned this time round; not as a reward or a failure but through physics, the natural laws of the cosmos – cause, effect and attraction. All memories, personality, knowledge and consciousness remain completely intact. In fact most often they are heightened. Nothing has changed other than the fact the body has fallen away and with it limitations that existed, sometimes in place for specific reasons.

No one enters back into the afterlife *omnipotent* or suddenly *all-knowing*. Each soul knows only what it has personally gained through lives lived so far. No one can know what at first it doesn't know or understand – just as on Earth. Sometime this applies to whole families. But that's the point – Earth is a place not only for enjoyment, exploration and experience – but for soul growth and fine attunement to occur, where positives and negatives blend together through personal will and discernment, so that when that lifetime is over, it affords each person the ability to move forward to new levels beforehand unavailable, but hopefully this time achieved. If a whole lifetime on Earth is lived without this higher knowledge, it's easy to see why we are stuck. We believed we just had to survive, to get through a lifetime in the best way we can – but that's all. Some people think we may continue in someplace called Hell or Heaven – but we don't yet have the knowledge to understand the reality of that. If a lifetime has been lived without soul growth, a whole lifetime will not have fine-tuned us to enable forward movement or progression. So when we return, if there's been little movement and we've accumulated more stuff called karma, we either have to return back to where we were last time, for now an intermediate level (or else fall backwards into shades grey or greyer), or may decide to rebirth as quickly as we're able to try again. It's really as simple as that (but as previously stated, rebirth is not often immediate).

No person wants to reach the afterlife and see what they've left unfinished, that they could have done better had they realised, especially when that knowledge was close. It's not very nice to see loved ones struggle, to see outpourings of pain and sadness or to watch them clear up what should have been done by ourselves.

Nothing in life prepares us for what is ahead. No teachings exist except through esoteric and religious renditions, but religion for many doesn't cut it. They instead steer away as far as they can from any trust, truth or understanding it could give/ represent, or the opposite becomes more apparent; many get too caught up in the words being produced to see the meanings each story represents. Some priests are too frightened to step outside the parameters of their own chosen faith just in case they are smote by life or the devil they speak of. But in truth they also are often too closed to the whole higher meaning itself.

No wonder in life we are where we are, because we've followed those before us with blinkers.

CHAPTER 12

Every person that came into this hospital did so because they were traumatised, not from their recent passing and what that produced, but because they were still alive. Shock is a better way to describe it. All were in shock because their lives finalised in a snap, in an instant. I can tell you – it is very disorientating. Not only that, some desperately try to get back, disbelieving what just occurred... The positive flip was that at least they were here in this place where help was at hand. I myself and many others were alone; what would happen next depended on what's needed next to continue their journey and to make their adjustment make sense.

In truth, although I didn't know it, even when I really thought I was alone I was still being looked after, but my helper was kept out of view. The proof was when peace washed right over me and I knew that I'd be alright. Every person is looked after in this manner, but generally we're oblivious to this happening.

First we must realise that we all have free choice and free will. Yes, other factors will come into play, but the decisions, choices and actions we take in each moment are our own. We must also remember that we have a soul contract, the contents of which will not always be apparent until after this lifetime is through, which also impacts on our pathways, our ability to choose and discern and our chosen life journey. How we process these things and build up a picture is dependent on personal choice too. No one holds power over us. If they do, then we've let them, through fear or sometimes perhaps being lazy. It's only when we get back to the afterlife realms that we can see the repercussions of those actions, but by then that change is largely too late to alter many things or to do something about them to make circumstances, situations and happenings better, different, more complete... But again, that's the point of this book, to help ordinary folk recognise they have an infinite spectrum of choices always at hand and that they'll revisit the result of all actions, u-turns, strengths and talents back here on return.

Back here, once people understood where they were and what had happened, they calmed down. Once calm and more peaceful, they went somewhere different, more in tune with their own needs and next steps going forward. Remember that this place was only a landing point, but for me it allowed realisation of what I'd dismissed at home. And my own understanding didn't stop there. I became better acquainted with the nun. It was she who gave me better insight in regards to religion and church.

To be a nun in the first place was to her more *a calling*, a need stemming forth from within to do good, to give back, to be of service to the *oneness* – to *God,* if you like, for the want of a better label or word. But on Earth we must realise that even though individuals set themselves up to stand for such things, they are human, and being human means they are fallible with the same flaws and abilities to do good or bad, to win through or fail – as we all do.

This calling didn't just stem from choices in this life – but from past lives lived, choices and karma as well. A deep movement or knowing is held by the soul, a knowing that it's part of something bigger, that it has a job/mission to do or to complete, so it looks for the best route to do it. Not all clergy come from this place. Some hide from life and from others because before they've been hurt or have done deeds that were far less than favourable/good, so they seek sanctuary or retribution for those acts. Remember many lives, stories and personalities play out simultaneously, all under the umbrella of religion. From the outside all we see is the packaging, the wrapper, the label of church, religion or service. We expect they are good because that's the projection they give to the world.

In truth they too are just people, in some cases with a bit of higher knowledge. But sometimes this knowledge is tainted by handed-down untruths and belief. Good does exist – but not always in the manner we think or are led to believe. Everything and everyone links to it unconditionally – we don't have a choice – because without that connection we would not by any means each have life. But then that good (or light) live connection can dim or fade through live deeds which are wilfully negative.

God is the totality of everything. Everything! God didn't make religion – people did. God doesn't say we must stand in worship or we'll be smited or struck out – it was the understanding of past people who didn't know any other way to put it – or who wanted riches, power or control for themselves – who said that.

In truth, God is a label – a name – just as I too have my name and you are given yours at each birth. How else could you be known or recognised without it? God is a name. A name for the Oneness, for the consciousness we're part of. Its essence is purity and love (unconditional love – the kind of which isn't really known upon Earth), which in turn is just positive energy, raw potential and live creativity tapped and untapped. It's life, vibrant and bristling with possibility – formed and unformed, with the knowledge of all that has been and is...

Religion was just *one* way to try to relay this message. Stories handed down by words – not even always by the people they portrayed. It was known these happenings were important so they were recorded later by those who could read, write and remember, because remember again, not many were educated. The power of word and actions, fear, punishment, reward and captivity were strong. God didn't make religion – people did.

Again I was getting the understanding I needed. It was beginning to make better sense. So that's why I was so opposed to religion... I thought it was because of bad priests, bad actions and experiences, but in truth the whole thing was much deeper. There was nothing really wrong with any particular church or creed – as people came together to share love and gratitude to *God* or such like, to the oneness of source/the universe. Their energies add together to create a much greater mass. This mass or good energy can then be added to more of the same – to aid or to help/uplift/contain/heal other things, but only if someone directs it. Too many are caught up within the words of religion and that's all. Many go to church and believe they are good just by that action alone. In the week, they behave how they want to. When Sunday comes along, they feel they are cleansed and that's how the process continues. But again that's not the whole truth...

Now I could see a different picture emerging. I was surprised at how even with all my intelligence I could have missed this one too. Everything was starting to make sense. Life is very clever. Just by placing me here and by doing this work, by seeing the things I lately had done first-hand, I was stripping back a lifetime of hurt and misunderstanding I'd unknowingly wrapped myself in.

I had let other people and outdated beliefs overrule me. As much as I'd thought myself in control – I was not. In life that would have been a hard pill to swallow – but here there was nothing to now push against. Truth was realisation and realisation then was cathartic, a healing elixir that made my existence feel better.

Funny how when you look back with more information that allows you a wider perspective, you can see what played out somehow differently. Much was making more sense. The nun being here whilst administering to her calling allowed me to explore things in life I'd been too angry to see. I had never liked being *told* what to do. I'd brought myself up from the depths of life's dealings when no one was there to even throw me a rope or support me... so to be told there was something I'd missed – I just couldn't swallow it, for I knew the many battles I had faced alone, with no one to understand or reach in. I'd been my own saviour and hero.

Every incident I was witnessing here was giving me more understanding. I could see myself mirrored back, except I could see that I was lucky – lucky that somehow I'd realised not too late there was more. Granted, too late to do something before my own passing, but not too late to do something now.

I was being offered a chance. No one had told me, but just like on Earth it was dawning, unfolding before me.

Everyone knows what they've been through and that deep inside they are good. But often in life, they're left trying inadequately to prove this, so instead of just *being,* the accent leaned more towards *action* in *trying to prove what you're worth.* That then creates the opposite effect because in turn you never feel recognised or appreciated enough. It's not that the world doesn't see you or that loved ones don't love you enough – but more that you don't know your own power. If you can't be at peace or whole from within then you're searching outside for what's lacking. It's a Catch-22 situation.

(I am I). I am the One, that part of yourself you're not seeing because you gave it away; you didn't understand or accept that connection. How can you feel whole and connected when you believe yourself lost or alone? (I am I).

CHAPTER 13

No one will try to make sense of the life you've just lived. You do that yourself.

A little while into being here, when you are strong enough, it is time for your own life review. Remember this comes in many ways at different times to each person/soul, depending on what's happened and what's needed next. This is my own experience; I have heard of others both different and similar.

A film of the whole of my life was played out – with me as the star – but also the spectator. I saw not only what I knew but also the many variables out of view: paths I could have taken but didn't and their *would have been* outcomes; the effect of my actions on other people and how they went forward from that; the people who had hurt me and what lay unseen behind those actions displayed, sometimes deeper than was realised, soul agreements we'd made before birth... Sometimes life itself sent in curveballs to help nudge or move us along when things were stuck. No one was judging. Alone I saw all this myself, but now also through new eyes, from perspectives that I was still learning...

All things within my life had wider implications and meaning. The thread binding it together was my need to feel loved and happy. But had I found what I'd been searching for? Every single thing said I had. I just did not always clearly see it at the time.

Nothing was ever withheld. Every want and need had been met. Happiness. Love. Money. Respect. Independence. Education. Understanding. Loyalty. Friendships. Relationships. Family. Freedom. Health. Strength. Fun. Success... I'd had plenty. I saw the good things I'd done but also the good aimed at me that I'd missed even when actually received. How others had put themselves out, not linked to work and general expectations alone, but personally at some cost to themselves. I had been lost in a sea of what I'd thought life had become and forgot that I drove it myself. That the journey was a joy, not a burden. I'd been stuck in the old *what life is* story.

Every person is living their own belief system. Their story comes mainly from that and what they make happen from what comes along. Not everything is always physically chosen. Sometimes circumstances appear to dictate the next option. Sometimes other people or what is expected takes over. Instead of leading and taking charge or free flowing, it's easy to feel more a pawn, pressured by requirements, expected outcomes and what's deemed appropriate or the obvious next step.

I was strong and did very little that others had asked if I could not see the need for it. But in truth, I had set my own boundaries. I rebelled against those then myself.

But what had my gains actually given me? I had plenty of memories that I recalled as good times and stories to delight friends and family. I'd achieved all my goals; but when I had done that... what should have felt good just felt empty. That's why we go from one thing to another and another to see if more happiness exists there.

(I am I). Every soul searches for what it feels it is lacking/missing. No one looks for what it already has. (I am I).

I saw how my character was formed. This film I was watching was interesting from the position of being detached. Forward and backward it could be rewound and re-viewed until I knew it inside out from all angles. Time had no meaning. I didn't get tired. I stayed there as long as I wanted.

(I am I). It is important to understand what happened and why, to gain the perspective of different traits, gifts and value from that recent lifetime. What will happen next also stems from that same place of understanding, when all is added to each soul's overall lifetime objective. (I am I).

Don't think that there is punishment or judgement at this point, for people who led bad lives go directly to a distinctly different place. Here (and in all areas) everything occurs with unconditional love and understanding, cocooned in peace. Not airy-fairy. No recriminations – just clarity, truth, kindness and support. Everything that happens is carried forward by each soul, so all we are, do, have been and have overcome comes back to aid or to hinder, to adorn us. Much is like a tally of achievements, win or lose, good or bad, but sometimes when we think that we've failed, we've lived karmically for others, so it's not always possible to see the complete process from the viewpoint within Earthly life. Things can be bigger – more people may be involved also, with issues and deeper soul agendas themselves.

How often had I stopped to think about what I was creating? About what I thought my life was about. In truth, I often didn't look too deep at all until later. I just lived. I wanted happiness and a good quality of life and to share that. This I'd had. But in the background, something always felt missing. I had a hole that couldn't be filled no matter what I did or how I tried. I was chasing my own tail but didn't know it.

I'd always looked at other people and they amazed me. Their stories and what they did seemed better in many ways so often than mine. They seemed to have an answer I was seeking, only when I replicated what they did or how they got there – it didn't hit the mark I expected. Nothing did. I was looking for my happy-ever-after. But nearly everything in life has terms, a price tag or conditions: much I can see now was illusion, temporary, an enjoyable at the time but short-term fix.

Through this wider overview I was understanding ME, maybe for the first time in my life.

(I am I). Before each life and after, the overall experience of recent content is assessed to determine what's been learned, put to bed, lost or gained, to decide the next direction that a soul will then take for its happiness, higher purpose/personal soul growth, recognition and achievements still to be fine-tuned/attained to move forward. (I am I).

CHAPTER 14

How we live and act physically in our lifetime on Earth becomes the foundations for the next life chapter or experience we will have. Nothing is ever lost or hidden from the soul perspective of ourselves. All has consequences, gains or losses somewhere else. We choose our parents for the start that being theirs will grant us, depending on tasks we choose to learn, invent, overcome, release or move through. I saw the real truth behind my parents' dreams and expectations as well as the storyline they'd lived and what we'd shared. When you're living in that story with them, you see just a half-baked picture from the version of the story put together by yourself, by society and sometimes even them. Not everything I'd carried forward was the truth.

So what is the point of living life?

It seems complicated when we live it because together we're still finding out. The world itself is crazy, not because it *is* but because the people who live in it have made it like that. From my perspective now, I can see so much that I wish I had been privy to while I was still living there. It's not that this information was withheld – but more that I couldn't see it. We miss a lot that's really in plain sight. A whole lifetime is not enough to rediscover, to remember, to then do something with that data to make a difference somehow that will last. Through the birthing process we forget who and why we are. By the time we understand, it's time to leave – that's if we've even woken up at all. But even then it's hit and miss because much of the population still lives as though in waking sleep, a journey of their making which they believe as their own total lot. Hadn't I too been the same while I had lived?

Love is everywhere – we just can't see it. We expect it and we give it but barely notice when it's returned because it doesn't look or feel how we are taught. Much of what hurts or drives us is also fuelled by love, or by its seeming lack, or by ourselves.

I'd lived many times before, but of course I didn't know it. The specifics of the ins and outs don't always matter unless you need to work through something underlying to finally overcome, release or make it better, or if you needed to have it with you to serve another purpose later on...

Most souls have had a mixed history of good and bad. They return to put things right, to grow or make a difference to something or for somebody. We all add to the human matrix of evolution and survival playing out. Life is not against us. Instead, much of what occurs is more for us. All we want or need is given to us to make us happy, so we in turn send happy signals (positive energy) back out to life. Think about it. When you are a parent, don't you do anything and everything for your children? When you make them happy, it makes you happy too – you can feel it. When they're sad or mad, you feel that also. Life does just the same for me and you.

(I am I). Everything you generate is mirrored back to you. (I am I).

People are the conscious, knowing, thinking record keepers of the planet. We're Earth's present caretakers. But instead of looking after it, instead of valuing, loving and revering it – we think resources are infinite when they're not, that much exists for nothing but for our own use... But that's not strictly true. All is there for us, but we co-exist as part of it, within and on the body of life's own living surface. Our numbers are expanding at such a quickening pace that if we don't look after what we currently have, we'll ruin the natural balance and Earth's ability to replenish what's been taken.

And not only that – blind actions individually create an ongoing larger collective mass. How often do we act through negativity? How often do we generate gratitude, love and positivity in return for what's been received, positivity being the fuel the planet needs directly from us to keep things regenerating and flowing? That's partly why we all feel so tired. We've been very needy. Very few send goodness back. Many think life is heavy...and because life gives us what we ask for or personally/collectively believe – so it is...

We birth, we die and rebirth, often in fairly quick succession, promising each time that we do so to make things better, to get it right. Each time we incarnate, we take up a vacant place that another could have used, of perhaps a higher calibre, meaning a being/soul/person more evolved/enlightened. It's our choice and personal right to try once more... but as we birth again we forget this. When will we understand this simple process?

Life is rooting for us – not against us. It tries its best to support, to assist... but we don't hear or listen – because we can't. Many haven't reached that point of understanding on their journey.

Don't get caught up in your story. Things will work out fine if you understand the process, the bigger picture of life's language playing out.

All that I had been through was there to help me and others grow, to help me overcome what I had chosen to move beyond, but it's easy to get stuck or caught up in the drama. I'd believed myself both hero and victim of my story: I thought I was always right because in the past I usually was. I stood in truth. But I had simply reached a ceiling within my own personal development. Because I didn't know this, I travelled round and around in circles in search of answers that were nowhere. I'd simply passed the goal posts that I'd set sometime before.

Life for most of us is a tale played out within two halves. The first is exploration of what it means to actually be here. We build the structure from a story that we create or tell ourselves life is about. At some stage we should complete that, which includes karma recreated and overcome. The next part is the reason for which we actually birthed – the part where we are happy and give back...

Everyone's so entrenched in giving in that first stage, but it's on a different level in a different way. No matter how good you think you are or what you may achieve during the first part of your journey – it still takes you to the same point of reaching that same ceiling. The first part is what you do with the physical aspects of your life, with building, growing, gaining, exploring, knowing, reaping, experience and survival. But when all needs are met and we have surplus, excess, it's only then for many that the next stage can kick in. But not many people at the moment can recognise this. Many instead hold tighter or grow further what they've built, fearing it might diminish or fall away. They place all value on this section and judge themselves as that – not knowing or understanding that they are more, that life has even more delights in store just waiting for recognition to begin...

This second stage (while still physical) is far easier – not harder...

My helper was again calling for me to go. I was ready for another stage of my own journey to now kick in.

CHAPTER 15

How can we live when we no longer have a body?

Earth requires physical form to allow us to function on its surface as we need or want to. It's only our body's matter that keeps us grounded. Without that, we can't remain. In life continuing beyond body's form – where I am now – I still exist. I am the same me, with the self-same character, memories and life experiences, only now they're much enhanced. Everything's clearer, a lot more intense. Pain itself has gone away because that links to body not to soul, unless its cause is more emotional, but that also falls away when you realise its true root cause or futility.

I still look exactly like me, but now more vibrant, happy and well. Earthly worries are non-existent because nothing can be gained through worry's presence – for now at least. Instead, I put all effort into processing what I've been through, lived, expressed, experienced over years. All had had its purpose – the bad was just as valuable as the good. This is not always apparent when you're living in the thick of what's unfolding, but nothing is ever wasted, even wrong turns or mistakes still carry merit because on the surface, when life seems stuck, growth's still occurring, something is working out. Change is always taking place on levels somewhere. The trick is to understand it and keep up.

It's funny how I now could see beyond things that had bugged or hurt me during life... How often do we go beyond our own emotions, beliefs, perceptions? Or step back from what is happening to take a break or even review our personal story? We're so busy surviving, building, living that we forget to check again why we might be here and what we've still to do. In the long run isn't that what part of the problem is with living?

From just a physical viewpoint, what really is the point of everything when we die and leave all behind us that's been built? But right now, here I am – and that's *not* all there is to life. Everything that really matters we do take with us: all creative efforts, dreams, achievements, aspirations and victories gained. Because nothing can be hidden, nothing vital is ever lost. All remains visible within the blueprint of each soul. But again the question *why* keeps coming up.

Every person, every soul is a work of art in their own right, all still learning and fine-tuning, perfecting and ever growing. All have complete control of their own experience: a unique expression of what it means to them to be physical and here, through individual creativity and will. No matter what we think – all souls are free…

Every single soul thinks itself at the very centre point of life – because it is. Each one is a universe in essence, connecting, collecting, exploring and inventing as it travels through the timeframe, space and energy continuum that it lives in. Information gained is uniquely processed/assimilated and sent back out again as more live and active data towards others, towards life. As good as it's always been, science accepted what was measured and provable but could not fathom what was physically not there – which to all intents and purposes was invisible. How can you explain what has no form or no property to measure? Mathematics works out equations that when added to experiments helps them add up to make sense, but equations are still not tangible as proof. You can't touch or see what they may measure when relating to what's actually not visible. And mathematics cannot explain or know the reasons *why*...

While still alive and physical I was locked into my own unfolding real time dramas – that place where no one really knows you, where you *are* the central star and you fight for understanding, recognition, survival, respect and much more daily. Where you rarely feel that you're seen properly. I'd been through a lot, which in my own internal world I thought was much more than my fair share, but what many of us forget is that everyone has a storyline that's really the backbone of who they are and where they've reached so far. It's just the story they chose to work through this time round, though while it's happening they forget and so don't know it.

Every person wishes to belong, to feel loved, happy, needed, safe and in some way important – that they matter. But situations can't always offer those things because in life these are not physical – so don't in actual terms exist. They drive us fundamentally but can't be held, touched, seen or measured: they're invisible; they fluctuate; vary; are different for one and all at different times; they are soul based. We're taught that they are nothing more than changing chemical fluctuations working in line with conditions/contradictions of the body, but if that really is the truth, then why do I have those very same feelings now? I don't have a body. Yet I do still think and move, feel, communicate, intuit and live life in the very same manner, possibly better than I had for a very long time.

Much that we unconsciously search for in life and in other people is really inside of ourselves: we just didn't know to make that connection because very few have done before. Nothing will work in the way you expect because people are not the problem. You are. I was. We all are... We get in our own way and then block our own potential. Believe that you'll be hurt and then you will be. Believe life is hard/difficult and that too will be. Whatever you carry inside that agrees with thoughts of personal lack – and your *less than you really are theory* is what you'll produce.

> (I am I) *Every soul is in charge of itself. I am not able to interfere because of free choice and free will. Interaction, no matter how small, would negate this. For live creativity to happen unencumbered, uniquely for each individual, the live soul itself must exercise free will. Limitations of body will then be reduced because soul naturally understands it's not body. Body is the servant to soul. Everyone thinks it's the other way around. Body is only a cloak that each soul wears physically temporarily.* (I am I).

CHAPTER 16

(I am I). Death is not death as you think it to be. Birth into body is a transition from one level into the next. It's soul as individual spirit (meaning a life without physical form), taking its place upon Earth for a limited period. Intelligent individuals choose to create and experience life on this physical planet. Remember that soul is immortal – meaning eternal – meaning always present – unending. Body isn't. How could this be any way other? (I am I).

First you must know that you don't re-enter life after physical death as completely all-knowing. For me, as for many, it's confusing to still be around. Even when you *do* manage to understand more, it brings what you've just been through – a whole lifetime lived – into question. The first thing we all ask is what it was really all for... I would have definitely been angrier had I not been assisted by those working on this side to help ease me back into my new life and its next stage. Everyone here works willingly to help for reasons relating to higher life, to their own soul improvement and growth. Most have been through lives on Earth physical but also didn't understand or correctly grasp the *larger world* process. Earth is a living biosystem within its own right. For us to live on it we have to have body/form, or just like steam we would drift. We choose to explore and experience all another lifetime can offer. However once you do realise this fact, it puts a completely new spin on the process.

I am still alive despite moving through death. I've spent time on Earth and departed – some might say too soon. That's true to a point. Had I known what I now do – or at least had I remembered even a bit – I would have taken better care of my body to make it last longer. (Ironically, this used to be one of my personal catchphrases, but back then I used it in jest...) But in the overall picture, had things been in anyway different I would not now be writing this book. When I was alive (so to speak) it would not have happened. Not only was I stubborn and shut – but I couldn't explain from this angle to contribute and help as I'm doing. I would not have believed it. But that's the tragedy. It's better to be open enough to explore these possibilities than to be stubborn and shut. A whole lifetime lived in a half-truth – regardless of how good or bad that life is – is a lifetime lived unaware of the cost and continuing result of our actions, not just individually but collectively. We live as though nothing else matters but getting through this one life, to last until old age in the best way – or any way possible.

I didn't expect to die when I did – but I also didn't expect to survive that. How many of us would? Remember that every experience is individual. What you expect during life, even subconsciously, is what you get when it's your time to cross over. Religious souls gravitate to an area where others carry their same held beliefs. If you believe you will drift as part of the universe – you'll get that, not because it's your destiny or punishment but because it's your right. You could float for what seems an eternity but at some point your soul would get bored. It would stir as you again start to question... That little flutter or crack or shift in mindset would be enough for life or understanding, recognition or live intervention, to enter, to get through to bring you back into line with the next opening phase of your journey.

Remember many levels of understanding, education, intellect, expectation and attainment exist upon Earth. Don't we see and know many ourselves? But infinitely more levels exist after life when you're no longer contained or held down by the body. *Earth is not the only planet teeming with life.* But it is the one closest to our own soul's live requirements for now.

> *(I am I). This information will not be easy for some to believe because it requires you to open up to a higher understanding of life. Instead of making this life less important, it helps to make sense of what you've so far been through. It makes your current life here the most important you've ever had yet. (I am I).*

I wish I had realised before. Once you die, your present story is over. There's nothing more you can do to fine tune or alter what's been left undone or unsaid. You also can't fine-tune your life force / energy / soul, which means you'll gravitate to the level that then fits you best – but no further without further growth. But even then you're still possibly growing/fine-tuning through the acts and vibrations you've left in your wake, through live effects you may have left still unfolding – good or bad…

In Heaven (so to speak, let's call it that) the purpose of being is to fine-tune your life force to get closer to a state of nirvana, of bliss. Every soul wants this. Imagine a state of permanent bliss, stronger than the state reached together when making love, a place without hurt or the search to find self, where you know absolutely you belong because you feel you've reached home. That's what the life force of every soul is actually part of. But we forget when we're born. Through countless incarnations of not knowing this truth, we become heavy with troubles and grow dimmer. On Earth we forget – but once body falls away we remember and if we're lucky we've achieved personal aims to be able to progress a bit further towards new levels this time.

Remember we get what we expect, depending on the quality of life lived that we've just left. Every soul gets what it's earned, not as punishment or prize but because of physical and natural laws of attraction, physics and cause and effect.

I now had to go. It was time for me to get back to work, not for money or gain but because it was part of my understanding and growth. In a nutshell, I was lucky. Not many souls/people get to learn as much as I have in a short space of time. I was being helped because in essence, I'd lived most of life according to truths and beliefs I had carried. I wasn't a saint, far from it really, but overall it seems that I'd worked right on something, this book itself still playing a part in that journey...

Daily more and more people arrived at the hospital, every one of them equally confused, shocked, angry or in deep denial... I'd been *soooo* not alone in what I'd encountered myself. Many different variations of after death experiences existed. But they all had one thing in common. Each person was shocked to be still living. Many more deeply wished they had realised before that their experience on Earth was to then set the scene for something else after. It would have given deeper meaning, even purpose, to what they went through or had wrestled or fought with during life.

Nothing more could be done for them here, once they accepted this place was a starting point they'd quickly move on from. I don't know where they went onto next because that was to them individual; I only know what so far I had seen and been part of myself.

In my own freer time I'd caught up with my family, with where they are now and what happened for them after passing. We talked about what they felt they'd gained or had learnt and what they now wanted. Most were happy to remain as they are — in a place of happiness and ease without trauma, pain, debt or worry interfering. They were living the lives they'd searched and worked for during life but felt they'd been robbed of or missed. None had thoughts further than that. In death (or in life continuing) they were still the same souls who put their own core happiness first. Even passing through death had not really brought change any further. No problem there – just examples of personal choice. Mum was happy also, but she worked on helping families grow personally in kindness and understanding. She was content. They all were.

Every friend that I'd known and lost was over here with me – even those I hadn't personally liked... We caught up, we played and had fun. Every once in a while we'd talk about things much deeper and in our own ways put the world we had known back to rights, just as a group of friends of like minds or differences would have done so on Earth. They too were much the same people as they had been before. Some had gone on further towards higher awareness and awakening – as I was still doing – but not all. This act seemed to be determined more by a calling of soul, of whether they were searching inside or out for the happiness they believed they deserved – much as we all do in life...

Everyone was happy. Life was good. They'd found their contentment and love and until some point in the future that this would change; what more would they then look for and why?

I was always different. I'd always felt different. Something inside had constantly spurred me on to search or reach out for more, but I didn't know what that *more* was or what it looked like. I'd needed to know everything, to push boundaries. This desire was little different for me here than it had been on Earth; I was still hungry for knowledge, understanding and experience. I wanted answers, explanations and deeper expansion, I had an insatiable yearning for more.

CHAPTER 17

When still present in body, I'd indulged in recreational substances for pleasure. I was definitely not a drunk, but I enjoyed getting drunk for its feelings and the closeness I'd shared with my friends. I'd also enjoyed weed and other things (but we'll talk about this further later). A proud man, I'd always been personally disciplined enough to keep all my commitments in order, so during what I then termed my *free time,* I played. I just figured out I deserved it as everyone was taken care of and looked after. This was my personal release from *adult responsibilities and stress.* I loved how during those times I then felt more alive, how my music seemed better, how I could hear every instrument and note – even the pauses between notes had meaning. I was loved-up and happy and didn't see any harm in doing these things as long as I was hurting no one and all business was kept up-to-date; my obligations had always been met.

Being a tall man meant that my presence was felt wherever I was. In truth, I was known as a joker. I played tricks that made people laugh and feel happy. I loved being with people. I had stories galore as one who'd pushed all boundaries further. Never a dull moment and never a wimp, I helped others toughen up and take charge. At every opportunity I pushed all to the limit for no reason but to prove that I could and so too could they. I took risks when no one else would, even only to shock, because in doing so I felt more alive. No one could accuse me of being boring.

But as life trundled on and youth fell away, responsibility and commitments created a seriousness I didn't enjoy, so to compensate I made sure I played hard in a bid to keep hold of my youthful, fun side. Alcohol and recreationals helped my release. As my adult retreated, my carefree, unhampered, funny, sharing, caring, daring side took over. Where was the harm as long as I didn't hurt anything or anybody? However what I didn't know – or in fact wouldn't see – was that I was really just hurting myself.

Personal details here are not important. But I didn't understand the nature of trauma and stress I had placed on my body, my family, my friends... I didn't know life had many higher, lower levels unseen with further consequences, or that more would affect me than I wanted.

No one had warned me of the unwanted effects of excess from recreational substances, beyond what's usually verbalised. You shouldn't because... it's bad because... or maybe they had but I couldn't hear – or plain wouldn't listen... I'm not talking about the hard stuff here, thank goodness (although that's even worse – much, much worse), but about what we consider soft, mainstream entertainment, harmless, recreational fun. We hear drink is bad because of health and the body, not to mention behaviours and the trashing of boundaries it loosens, but no one has told us by way of plain speaking what other effects it can bring.

If you too are very down to earth, stubborn or earthbound you may not believe even this (but you might at least ponder the possibility), but I was living the same way as you before one day in the night-time – I died, completely out of the blue. I too didn't believe or want to know anything about energy, auras, hocus-pocus gobbledygook rubbish. I was a tough person, streetwise, resilient, strong, a survivor/leader and therefore I wouldn't be swayed.

Without going into the subject too deeply – while we're alive we are two parts – soul and body overlapping. Soul houses the body – not the other way around – but without soul the body has no life, no personality, no movement or animation. Body is just a working machine that keeps you (and all systems) moving and living as you want to.

As we ingest alcohol or substances, we enjoy a release. For a while we let go of parts of ourselves to have fun. We believe it makes us relax, and in some ways it does as certain brain receptors turn off, get muddled or fuzzy. Inhibitions tumble away as we are braver and freer to do what we want to as we feel less beholden to our usual self. But that *gain* is part of the problem.

Let's digress for a moment. Earth has a protective layer around it that we call the ozone. This layer prevents things unwanted from entering. We too have protection around us – to similarly prevent unwanted things, entities/energies from entering or remaining too close. This protection does have other functions also – but it keeps safe a layer of energy called aura. Aura is your own personal life force which extends beyond you (which if you could see it with your Earth eyes looks like the image in children's cereal TV advert, Ready Brek – different colours, extending out beyond your form in layers – like rainbows do in the sky).

We've already discussed how you waited a long time to birth here – that conditions had to be exactly correct to give you the start you requested depending on what you needed to achieve with your life.

So, your aura is part of your energy system. Protection extends to all aspects of your visible and invisible self all at once. Remember – not every soul in existence now has a body. I don't, but I still am writing this book. Not every soul, whether living on Earth physically – or out of body – is good, nice and kind. Many are not. Some are troublesome, disruptive, angry, sad – even evil (but again not always in ways you might think). A soul can only be what it has been so far – not just in one life but through many lives overall that it's lived. If it is bad then it will often stay bad until somehow it can be turned around. If a soul enjoyed trouble while it was here, if its *happiness, heaven or pleasure* (to all intents and purposes) was in gambling, or it fought, stole, drank or took drugs to excess – and more besides – before death (unless it thought itself broken or lost), then it still will enjoy, want those things after death, especially if it hasn't yet overcome them. Remember we go to the level that our soul fits the best at that time, not as punishment but as cause, effect and attraction. More often, we'll land first in rehab. There we'll have every chance to move away from and work through these behaviours if we want to, because mostly they link more with body. But we'll actually have to want that in the first place... We don't all become saints when we pass.

But here is the thing: in the afterlife realms, there is no need to drink or to eat unless we specifically want to because we no longer have a body to maintain. All we want is available. But nothing is as solid and permanent as on Earth. All seems to remain solid until it's no longer required and then goes just as quickly back into energy/ether...

When willingly you systematically partake in substance abuse, even the abuse of alcohol, beyond losing the senses, you are in danger of harming your aura. Not only that, because willingly and by free will you loosen yourself from your body (so to speak), when your mind and senses wander, you leave room for other beings to come closer or to step into your space and hold tight – beings who like/miss the buzz of activities in which you're partaking. They can't get the same effect when they're not on Earth physically (some even have never moved on) – so come in close to aid and enjoy your current actions. Think about it. Don't we do the same thing while living on Earth when we mix with our friends and larger groups? The more people gather together, the bigger the buzz, the better the evening or night. This doesn't alter because we have died. Instead it's enhanced. Remember life still exists. I am proof. There is proof all around. Those without form who are so inclined are attracted to those here with body – so they can share in their enjoyment, live energy and good times produced. You may have seen friends or have family who seem to alter completely the moment they drink or take drugs. It's because in reality – they do. One or many souls can often come in extra close which like the old Catch-22 helps everyone's enjoyment (or anxiety) occur that much more easily, sooner and more deeply.

This is not possession. Possession is where another entity takes over completely. This is not the same thing – but it's still not a good thing that it happens. It's even worse that while we're alive, we don't know it's occurring – that no one has told us and that through our own actions via free will – we allow it.

Sometimes souls/entities remain with you. They can get stuck or caught up in your aura's own magnetic field, or they don't want to move on to lesser or greater extents. You do have a guardian, believe it or not, but they can't override your free will. When you allow other energy life forms to get too close (without strict conditions) you can take on their behaviour/ characteristics as well. Compelling and other addictive behaviour applies here, and so too sometimes anger, depression, insecurity, over-sensitivity, feelings of being helpless or hopelessly lost (but not all). Knowing this stuff is not an excuse to do more of the same. Instead it's given to help you understand a little better what is going on, or around you, happening regularly out of usual attention/view.

The present body you have is a highly prized possession, because without it you can't retain physical life. Those who enjoy trouble or mischief want nothing better than to create havoc because they feed from and enjoy negativity. Like a virus/addiction, they live only to create more and more – because in lowering the vibration, only then do they really feel comfortable.

Here generally in life, after bouts of release (after said events), your senses come back to where they should be. It depends on your own strength of character as you pull yourself back together, so to speak. But when body dies there's nothing to inhibit, to pull you back or to keep you in check or on course any more, because happiness takes hold. Whatever aspects of life you enjoyed and practised the most while on Earth often become dominant until at some point you get fed up and you change it. That's how the afterlife operates. You create your desires or gravitate automatically to the level during this life you've attained. There still is a lot more to it than that but for now you should be getting the picture.

When I was alive, I thought Heaven would be boring if it even existed at all. I would rather go to levels where I'd have the most fun than be bored or boring – like my impressions of church or religion or do-gooders. But I was granted a glimpse of the highest of those lower levels. It was uncomfortable to me and not how I thought it would be. Souls were locked into their activities, feeding off one another in terms of enjoyment and goading, unaware about anything but their ongoing actions. It was grimy and darker and unkempt (remember I was already in a fairly good place). Standards of everything were lower. I didn't belong there, but I saw how easy it was to get trapped, to stay caught up or stuck. On earth in a body we enjoy all the pleasures we do – but what keeps things in order is perspective and time, morals, self-discipline and the knowledge of when things should end. On the lower life levels, you will do what you want for as long as you want and for as long as it pleases. Everyone's there for the same reasons, so the whole thing continues unhampered. Higher life beings don't belong there – even I – and I was no saint. It's up to each soul individually when it will realise that better exists – but it can't move forward beyond what it has physically earned without help from assisting higher beings. It's only in a body – while living here physically that growth of any kind is made permanent. It's where we raise and lock in our vibrations. That's why being physical on Earth is so important.

You can glimpse the idea of this knowledge when you think about your own life lived so far. How much of schooled learning did you retain? When you read a book (not about something you love –

but more generally) or you hear information – remember you're bombarded all day – how much is retained, even when at the time it's deemed useful? What's not used or recorded goes back out to the ether. It's forgotten or lost (even though it's recorded by soul). You only retain that which is used, that which is grounded or challenged. This truth affects you even more so when body has gone. What you are, you retain. What you've gained remains with you. Everything becomes visible in your aura, in your colours/shades/hues and how dim/bright your personal light shines.

(I am I). Earth is the matter that grants you a physical life. It supports and sustains all your own earthly needs until your body can no longer uphold you. This link then falls away, the soul will detach (the silver thread of life that links soul to body will detach) to begin the next stage of its ongoing journey. (I am I).

CHAPTER 18

What you are learning here is not new – quite the opposite, it's ancient. It's been shared before many times in many ways. Yet as the world clearly shows, we're no further forward in terms of understanding ourselves and the journey we're living than we were many centuries ago.

I am writing this book because when I was alive I would not acknowledge that any part of it was truth. I was wrong and I don't want to come back to live the whole thing again just to get back to the point I am now. I want to go forward in different ways because I've fulfilled a higher purpose in this life. Granted I no longer have body, but I have this link with my wife who can write what is now being shared/channelled...

God/source/the universe didn't make religion. Man/womankind did. People did it to people to teach/share higher knowledge at a time when few could read or write. Knowledge is handed down, or it gets lost or changed and forgotten, but in that hand-me-down process, a bit like the children's game of Chinese whispers, things get altered or taken out of truth context. Over time, people even changed words to wield power. They decided what could or could not be shared and how it should be portrayed to retain the most supremacy/control. Even biblical dates are not totally correct. They're nominated days to allow us to celebrate together. In the Christian calendar, how could Easter possibly change? This important occasion is on a different date, even a different month, every year. No one really cares about the date change but in many other ways, what's recorded in the text is taken too literally. That's what causes trouble and wars. Every religion believes theirs alone is correct. But that's not so. Remember God/source/the conscious life-force we're all part of did not say we must all be this or that. Humans did. Geographical location and historical times did (although miraculous teachings, happenings and higher guidance really still do occur). Each denomination is just one single facet, one path or one route up a very high mountain that we pass on our journey to reach the top peak.

If you believed in religion, when you pass over beyond death you gravitate to levels in keeping with those same held beliefs, not because they alone are correct but because that's what your soul has attained. You could live for millennia perfectly happily not knowing that more life exists. Even on Earth, the same truth applies for we see it play out the world over. A hundred years can pass for some who will change very little in views, thoughts, beliefs and behaviours. So in Heaven – where there's even less need to grow beyond where you fit or feel happy – it's possible to remain the same even longer.

So if we're happy, why do we need to change anything? Why should we grow or move forward?

Take a good look around you at physical life, at the stage we're all at and at states we're now trying to fix. We did all of these things to this earthly plane ourselves. Look at how we treat one another. Look at the murders and crimes that exist because people believe they only exist for this one life alone, that if something occurs out of view it is hidden, or if knife/gun crimes are committed – once the culprit is caught, that is that. But actually, it really is not that. Karmically speaking, these things can continue life after life after life until someone realises, stops the repetition and the whole thing is somehow worked through... Heaven and hell are real places that exist that we reincarnate from again and again... When someone is murdered, they don't puff away. Their life force continues – so they still exist. They just no longer have the cloak of their body.

Everything a soul does is recorded forever. Nothing is missed. At some point all will be replayed – again this is fact and not myth. People just don't understand that each life we live feeds/filters back into life's own living mainframe as input. We are responsible for all that is happening around us within real-time while we live there. After death, when that input is reviewed and worked through, we can see what we gave, produced, hindered or gained, angered or soothed, what we personally achieved or were responsible for or for what we could have changed but we missed – in terms of what we shared or created.

> *(I am I). This doesn't occur only at death. For the whole of a lifetime, each soul is connected to life. There can be no disconnection even after death because consciousness and life are not physical. They can't be contained, made or measured and they equally can't be snuffed out, obliterated. Life is a total intricately balanced conscious system. Nothing on*

Earth exists apart from this matrix. Systems are all forever joined. I am the sum form of that totality Myself. (I am I).

People think birth and death are the beginning and end of a lifetime, that the bit in between is down to advantage, to good or bad luck and all else that it takes to build up a life. Maybe that's part of the problem. They are not taught that all you are and have been remains with you; that we birth many times over again to try to be better than before. They believe they must fight their way through to get by, unaware that life responds and works with them. You can't be part of a whole working system but disconnected and alone at the same time... Connected or not – in this we don't have a choice. We exist before birth – we just don't have a body as we know it today – and we return to that same state after each life is individually finished.

What happens between birth and death is free choice depending on how we put things together. To be alive on Earth physically is a gift. We just forget that along the way. We come back every time to do better, to undo what we too helped create. But through the process of birth, amnesia kicks in and we slot into the drama we believe is the whole story complete. We get caught in dramatic unfolding of who did what to whom, why and how, of hardship and struggle and untruths.

(I am I). What you birthed into you are given to overcome and to grow forward from. Birth limitations give you an initial understanding of current earthly life that may be used as a springboard to jump higher. Why would life really be any way different? (I am I).

CHAPTER 19

I was lucky to have been the person I am, otherwise things could have ended up very differently. I was one who had egged many other people on to the point of them getting into trouble with their wives. I forced everyone around me to have fun. But in truth it was only because life can get too heavy when you don't grab it by the horns, live and use it while you can. Everyone thought me the life of the party, but in truth I was not always that person. Somehow in early youth I lost parts of myself that never really quite gelled back together. We make life so much more complicated than it needs to be...

I was now venturing out further afield. What we think of as beautiful when on Earth pales into comparison here. How can I explain the indescribable – other than to say you'll get to see it one day for yourself?

My job had now changed. I was able to assist in other areas where people had taken their own life. Not all had intended to do the job well – sometimes in a weird twist we believe *we'll show someone we're serious* about topics that hurt very deeply – sometimes it's more the old *seeming last straw* that broke the camel's back scenario. The problem now, though, was that once the deceased person had succeeded, there was no going back – even when help was close at hand. Suicide is seen as a final way out, but no one expects to survive – but survive they all do in life after death – but of course once again without body. What's more, it is often then clearer that other choices/alternatives were available. It's then appropriate to witness the pain of their loved ones because of the very nature of that actual act. Out of the two places that I had now worked – this one was harder for me. I could feel their personal sadness myself. I had even felt it at times whilst alive – I'm sure we all do...

Victims of suicide face the deep heartache and pain of what they did and of watching their family cope or get by when their physical presence would have made a big difference. To watch the repercussions and ripples of something you've caused is not easy. It's not true that they go to lower levels to pay for their act (unless they do so because on some level they believe they deserve it. Free will, personal blame and unforgiving deep beliefs can be powerful. This changes only when time shows that it can) – but it is true they must live with what happened. Life on Earth is seen as a privileged gift when you're living in realms without form. It's possible to see way beyond what occurred and what could have been done at soul level to alter a life path or direction. Not only that, they see how others then had to overcome what was left. They see the difference between how life should have been compared with what occurred from that point instead. They know the soul agenda they signed up to accomplish, which of course will remain incomplete, and the effects of that non-action on other parties or life's wider picture because something only they could have done will be missing.

Remember that each soul holds a record of all actions. It might be deemed necessary for their own personal growth to repeat some or the whole process over – to then take better options and complete what only they can. It's not always necessary, but often likely by choice for many depending on reasons and what occurred next for all parties.

From the perspectives of life we are now discussing, it's clear that each person has a function, a purpose unique only to them. If those tasks are not finished – a hole will remain that others must work harder to bridge.

Life on Earth is just part of the picture of us. We are alive before birth. We rebirth as pure unclouded, unshaped souls in new bodies to try again at establishing a good life. When that lifetime is through, we rebirth once again back into energetic spiritual existence.

So why do we keep coming back?

That's so easy to answer given the infinite possibilities of all you could be in a lifetime. Of course we'll come back – because we want to... (But some souls will want instead to go off to explore other directions, other realms and realities. Again energy vibrations will pay a big part as to whether they'll be able to do that.)

We birth into a place of existence most in keeping with what we have gained, lost, done or left undone during lifetimes before. In an ideal scenario, we'll manage to wake up to higher truths in time to accrue what we need before physical death. When that happens, at least then we won't have to repeat the main parts of the journey all over again before managing to reach that same point next time round. But even better than that, we will have managed to start work on our higher soul pathway much more quickly – being the real reason we birthed physically in the first place. When life is then finished, we'll see what's been achieved from a higher viewpoint perspective. We'll be proud. Perhaps we won't need to return quite so quickly to put right what before we had missed. We'll be more able to choose when we'll return, coming into a world that's worked much of the darker stuff out in the meantime. As things stand at the moment, many souls choose to return fairly fast to give themselves another chance to do better. I know which of the two options I would prefer if given the choice...

Before my own death, I was a stubborn man. I wouldn't admit that I was thinking of truths I was seeing within my wife's work. It's not easy to be proven wrong and then to admit it when you've carried the hate towards it that I did. That's why I insisted that my mum collect me. It was my own way to challenge this and to be proven once and for all whether it was right or wrong. This book is my evidence that these things are indeed correct. It's my own way to correct what in life I'd argued against. Not only that, it will help me move forward to new levels I now want to explore. I don't want to come back to repeat what has passed. If I come back at all, I want a clear slate to make choices without karmic attachments beforehand.

Most of my friends will not get to read this – but if you are one of them – take a fresh look at what's really around you. Be open to possibilities that this stuff might be true – then work out what that means for you.

My wife's books and wisdom will help you – and if not hers then there are still plenty of others. Find the reasons you have lived through what happened for you and redraw – readjust and enjoy the time you have left.

Never underestimate your personal power and potential. Begin to notice the directions you feed into life and its answer when it reflects back.

Remember – everything is always recorded. This is not to make you buckle in shame or pain – but meant instead to help you grow as you change things around for the better; for the betterment of you and for life. Most people feel empty inside, regardless of growth or standards of living achieved. They've reached a ceiling, a point they then question what this life is all for – but instead of being a problem – it's a good thing. It means you are ready for a new level of growth to occur. You have been through the hard stuff already. When you realise your potential and how life itself works to support you, the rest comes. It will flow in when you are able to let it.

Don't be like me and wait until it's almost too late. I am lucky my wife can connect and do this bit – for the purpose of what this book will then bring.

Everyone will have their own unique life experience once their time frame on Earth has worked through. By being open to higher truths, you'll be happy that this book came to you.

Remember – this is not religion. Whatever you are, you are still free to be, but instead it's about how you connect with and use better the present. Be more aware that you alone write the script of the unfolding life story you are living. Don't be a bully, don't be a victim – don't think that where you are is the sum of your lot – nothings for nothing. Instead it's a phase, a time and place that soon passes, regardless of whether it's good or bad.

While you have time – once your basics are met – begin to notice what you wish you could alter or change, fine-tune, help or redraw, to leave as your own mark behind you in terms of the wider world picture. Do some of the things you always wanted to but never have…

Money is good to afford what you need – but excess and waste you'll become ashamed of if you don't use it wisely. Don't give it all away – because you are not a wallet/purse – but put it to good use to assist something that attracts your attention, that calls to your own soul agenda and purpose. Be wise. Don't just give it to the first thing you see – look deeper. Make sure it will be used properly.

Know your potential and purpose...

> *(I am I). No one will judge you more harshly than you'll judge yourself when your present lifetime is over. Not because you need praise or something opposite – but because you've affected your own growth and ability to move forward – or not. All you'll then be dictates the quality of life you'll have or birth into next time. Do you want to go through this whole stage again?*

> *Never before has life been so open to change to aid and assist all endeavours the way it is now. You have a real opportunity to work with it.*

> *A new way of being is occurring and you can be part of that process. Like a phoenix – or a hybrid – you are much more than right now you may know. (I am I).*

CHAPTER 20

Waking up to a new understanding will not change you into something that you're not. You've lived countless lifetimes already to get to this same point of enlightenment. Not only that, life has waited long for you to do that.

Putting trust into life to help you then live it can be strange, almost hard, when you've never personally tried it before. It can be difficult enough to trust yourself in the first place, but then putting faith into something unseen and unmeasurable for some goes against the grain of common sense.

(I am I). What would you lose with being open to explore this possibility? At the moment, you may believe that you're singular, operating alone within the framework of your chosen life. But what if much more than you realised was available, operating just out of view alongside you to lead, to help, assist? What would it mean if this was right for you to now explore that? Each person has the right to try every avenue and pathway that exists. Everyone has the same chance to be happy, not only on physical, work, love and home levels but on higher soul growth, contentment and happy ever after – nothing will be left undone that can be completed levels. Earth wins. You win. It's really as simple as that. (I am I).

I had to work hard to reach this place of understanding. Not because it was difficult but because it was outside my current scope of activity and usual thought attention. It made sense of what I'd experienced and what is behind what's occurring in life. Each aspect of life is in shake-up, wake-up mode. For evolution to occur, life has to drastically shift. Sometimes these things happen slowly over time, almost unseen and unnoticed. But we humans have brought this shift forward. We live hard and fast. We've altered the natural structure of what happens, when. Living in the fast lane – we've also now too fast-tracked life.

This is not good or bad, but just how life is today. We have to understand a bigger picture to make sense of what should occur. If you're fighting for survival from inside any problem – you'll never reach solutions because all that's in plain sight is more negativity. Step back, rise higher, levitate and see the overall view. See all aspects available, but remember they start with you too, with your own interactions, expectations, aspirations and day-to-day habits, activities and acceptance. What you live, believe and buy into stimulates and then expands everything else.

Many will not explore what you will take much further. If they reach an understanding that repercussions do exist for day-to-day behaviour, it may stay with them long enough to then live better. The concept of an eye for an eye is old-fashioned. How can good come about from two wrongs? It's better to understand that what we each do to another we do also to ourselves – if not today or tomorrow – then in the karma we'll attract next time around.

Karma is the natural outcome of accrued occurrences. What's not completed, corrected, healed or worked through keeps repeating until it is no longer necessary. To birth on Earth physically and to live through these events is the only way they can complete. Only on Earth can growth, change, better choices and corrections be accessed.

(I am I). Earth is the body of what has been called conscious mind. You have a body yourself. Yours comes, goes, changes, grows and evolves over time and lifetimes experienced. Why then is it strange to suppose that I have the same? I am real. I am alive. I am life in its entirety. Without this connection, you would not exist. Without what is your own eternal life force – your own living soul – you would not be conscious. Yet you are consciousness, having a real time experience. You own your own individual existence, your life force, your memory, ability and personal identity. I Myself own the whole complete thing.

Within, you have cells. All individual. All working and playing their own part to keep body in perfect order. No one programs or tells them what to do. It occurs. It happens automatically. All works as it should – unless it does not. I am the same. I am the totality of life – of conscious life; you yourself are one part of that, as though one working cell. You are individual, unique, inspirational, evolving and manifesting all at once, operating singularly as though alone, but really inventing, exploring, discovering, understanding, enjoying and living the whole complete thing. Without human beings who would or could give meaning to life? All would exist, but how would it be known?

Earth is the original Garden of Eden. Nothing religious is contained within this truth. This is just fact.

Earth was born. It happened. In terms of measured time, you already know the time scale and physical process – but remember time is only relevant in your present understanding. Miracles exist. Things can happen instantaneously – or take a long time – so time is not all you perceive it is even now. Earth happened. You have proof because you are living on it.

Originally, all was positive energy. You can liken that to all new life forms birthed. Love and positivity are the very same thing. No negative action or thought had yet birthed. Humans arrived. They were no different to any other life force until they accessed understanding and knowledge. It was here that duality came in.

The first negative thought set in. Fear and contradiction were born. Fear became action and action behaviour – which spread. You can still see the likeness today when innocence does not see bad intent coming. At the birthplace of fear and uncertainty, the very first time, life was still love being open and innocent. Negativity had just occurred for the very first time. It birthed and then became grounded by action – which then became form. Take a glass of pure crystal clear water. Take a droplet of ink and place one drop at a time into the glass of pure water. Over time the water will change. Earth is the same. It needs humankind to wake up, to realise this mistake and to come back into recognition of what's happening. (I am I).

CHAPTER 21

When I first passed over (as in death), I was shocked. Shocked at the occurrence itself... I was there on the bed. But I was also standing there alive by the bedframe. I could not get back. I was unsure and panic set in. What was going on? No warning was given. I had lost my place upon Earth... Thousands of things passed through my mind: questions, facts, figures, information I'd accessed or heard. What was going on? What had I missed or done wrong? The act of how I'd just died and the occurrence of unfolding activities relating to that fact were not as important as what was occurring personally for me – was this real or was I going to wake up?

Everything kicked off around me, just as you would expect, but I was not in my body. I couldn't get back into my body. I was dead but I clearly was not. Everyone wonders what dying is like. It was easy. I had just stepped away as you would step out of your slippers. Even that required action. For me, there was no action. I was asleep – then I wasn't. I was in bed – then I wasn't. I was standing, yet my body was dead. It's the strangest experience – almost like the shock of an unexpected slap to the face.

With that shock comes thoughts of disbelief, of the panic of what you're going to do. What should I do? I didn't know. I was unprepared. How could you prepare for what before that moment to you was still unknown?

Events unfolded physically as you'd expect they would. For me, though, I was alone. Being alone was always the worst thing for me. I was not good by myself. I'd always needed company. Looking back now, I wondered if I'd always carried the knowledge of this moment in my soul... Did some part of me always know it would come? Who can tell? How much do we know of events written that we have to pass through? Was this part of my karma? My life plan? The agreed destiny I said I'd take on? These questions are mine now as I look back. They were not mine as things unfolded back then...

In life, we question what we're living for. We question life's purpose and meaning. Even here, I was questioning again. I'd already learned so much and understood more about what I had been through so far. I'd been granted insight to levels beyond what I had wondered about. Even the wider scope of religion I could somehow get – but I was still needing more. My soul was still hungry. I had not found my completeness, my inner peace yet. Knowledge was filling the void. Like a sponge, I soaked everything up. I was still hungry, still searching, still stirring. I hadn't yet met my potential, found where I fit, my own place.

Was this it? What was I missing or lacking?

(I am I). When a soul first returns back to spirit (into levels of Heaven or life continuing thereafter) it must make sense of what it's just lived through. This will happen in many different ways depending on individual souls. No two will be identical – just as each life on the planet can't be either. Time will not exist at this point, for time is a relative concept held by people to help them with being physical.

Each soul will remain in the learning, un-learning, remembering, overcoming, understanding, forgiving and recognition phase until it no longer needs to. No rush.

No schedule to meet or delay. Existence and purpose are suspended for now to allow personal insight to adjust. This is rebirth back into spirit. Depending on receptivity, the quality of life just lived and individual awareness of divine, higher attainment of truths, souls will pass through this stage easily or not. Not because of underlying pressures of law and punishment but because of each soul's ability to accept the role it too played within life and situations it just left behind. Because many feel victimised or short changed during life, they will need to accept failings as well as triumphs that presented. (I am I).

Many people live in a storyline they create. Not all are happy. Many make do. Others still don't, but regardless of what they believe, they need to change and change what they do; life trundles on much the same. One storyline's swapped for another. How can you find your true happiness when you keep searching outwardly in the opposite direction away from it?

(I am I). The true gift of life is the journey that will go wherever you lead. Every day is an open new page. Nothing exists on it except what you put there yourself through interaction, deeds and commitment. Only you can spend your own life force. Your will

is free will – again you can choose how to use it. You're at the mercy of no one. In most countries of the world, you are free to express and explore.

From a higher perspective, as if you were now in the after-life, take a look at what you've made of life so far, not from a perspective of limitations and believing you've been unlucky or somehow held back – but from the perspective of your storyline expressed so far and of the distance you've actually come. Recognise old dreams and goals you once set and again see how you've surpassed them. Notice what's left to be done.

It's important that you don't fall back into a negative state here. No one is judging – for there's nothing to judge. You are the keeper of you. If you like what you can see, then great – well done and continue, but if like many you're not pleased – be glad that your life is not over, that you have time to turn it around. Don't blame anyone for misfortune or for dealing the life cards that were dealt. No matter what happened, it's all in the past. How much longer will you carry it with you? What does not fit in the day you're expressing – let it go, put it down, make adjustments and move on. No blame. No judgement. Move forward. Use the day you are in to its own highest purpose and good. This is not about running from aspects of life you don't want or like any more. Take small steps and change what needs changing, but do it with soul. (I am I).

CHAPTER 22

I was seeing a pattern of unwritten blame that we carry. No one is responsible for your thoughts and actions but you. I was the same. I had looked at my life and I was the hero. Yes, I could perceive my mistakes loud and clear, but I also kept logs of my goodness. Many times I'd been hurt because others hadn't seen the real me or known how I'd overstretched or put myself out to assist or accommodate more than I supposed was my share. But what was my share? What was fair? When had I done too much? When had I done much too little? In an attempt to do better or good or feel nice, how often had I done much too much at perhaps the wrong time, perhaps in the wrong way, only to feel my attempts were not recognised or even appreciated? How often had I leaned on others too heavily when in fact I should have done things myself?

What I carried inside was not always the actual truth of the moment. More often it was a version, a supposition/facet of fiction. What was real and what was made up? Sometimes in life I was so wrapped up in feeling my story I forgot to have a check in on myself. In the game of survival and growth we learn to look forward, to eat or be eaten first. How far we go before we realise how little we need...

In the afterlife, these things and more are called into question, but when you're here, there is no one to blame or pin anything onto. You see what you gained from all life experiences and what in turn life itself gained from you.

If we do birth many times to try to be better – then what had I learned or given back? What parts of life had been better because of the fact I had been there?

> (I am I). Again, don't spiral down into pain or depression. That's really not what this is about; like a game of connections you feed into life, but life and other people connect and feed also into you. It's what you make

of all eventualities that's important. How you turn things around for the better. Your life is just your story so far. Family and friends are going through the same growth as you. Your own love and happiness are not solely in them – but in you. You all search for the same from each other instead of realising that these things are in you. Peace and tranquillity stem from within. Love and happiness are produced from the self. When you feel these things, you connect to the same things without... Life reflects back what you generate. (I am I).

Already I wonder – but what about war? What about innocence and bad deeds that anger and create fear, loss or pain?

(I am I). These are not part of love nor of you – unless you are the cause. They are the product of that very first grounding way back in time when the first thoughts of a negative nature were produced.

Just like the ink dropping into clear water, the water becomes cloudy, but the same pure crystal water still exists there. Life is the same way for people... A negative act added to a negative act will not cancel it out but make it larger. Law and order is a good thing, but only when it's truthful, when it prevents things from happening again and allows for learning, healing, understanding, growth and a complete turnaround shift. But in many cases, that's not really what happens.

Personal responsibility is the key. What each soul produces, it has responsibility for, if not openly in this life then karmically for many lives later.

What you see playing out on the surface of Earth is the ripple of actions – the cause and effect of millennia. A millennia of people locked into their own supposed stories. Cause and effect impact all in their path, not just those who set deeds into play. You can see the evidence as you look back along the story you've lived. How often were you caught up in responding to circumstances and events you had little to do with? How often did you act out of character, outside of morality, good judgement and truth? How often did you blame other people? How often did others blame you?

All these things and more are simply a drama unfolding and continuing to play out with you as a chess piece – a pawn. Yet in truth you are worth more than that.

Every day is a gift that stands alone in its own right. You have lived and used many but just a handful stand out as special or in some way defining to you or to history. (I am I).

CHAPTER 23

People wonder what Heaven is like when they're alive still in body on Earth. Most suppose it's better. But once in Heaven, many want to return back to Earth for all that being here means. There's a yearning in soul to be more, to have and attain more, to learn, know and grow, to evolve. This yearning is not only on Earth. In other realms too, conscious mind wants to ever explore. Peace, love and contentment are different. They exist when all needs are met.

We have proof that Earth was born. To all intents and purposes it was and still is a garden. Everything existed in a well-balanced way until people birthed also. No other life form needs, takes, uses and wastes so many resources. By itself this isn't a problem – but as population numbers increase to become larger masses – problems are now being seen.

People are searching for answers and meaning in their own existence. But if you only look outwardly, you'll miss what's occurring within. Not physically, because remember that your body is a complex brilliant self-contained bio machine. It lasts as long as it can, but only as long as the life/force/soul stays attached. When soul detaches, body cannot support itself any more beyond its natural working purpose. So looking inwards is not to understand the intricate workings of body – but to know your real self – the things that drive and propel the real you. These things exist nowhere in body. Instead, they are aspects of soul.

You and your soul are the same thing. Not you and your body, because body will at some point fall away. If you regard yourself only with your present form – when you lose it, what do you have left?

I am as ALIVE right now as I was when I was there, still living. Everything changed from the moment I travelled through death. I had to question all I thought to be true. Even beliefs I didn't realise I carried came into view because in life they had programmed me too.

In life, people strive for survival and physical things that will free up time and help ease the strain of mundane and heavy repetitive chores. This is good – but only to the extent that you've freed yourself up to achieve or enjoy something useful. Everyone wants a better lifestyle – but this still only falls into the survival category. You are alive for more than just survival. Yes, basic needs should be met. A fair exchange for a good day's work is every person's right. But to the cost of exploitation and of the unique capability of others – that's not the way to do business.

Because we've forgotten the reason we came here to be – we got caught in life's prevailing stories. How we choose to interact is by free choice but only to the point that we recognise more choices exist.

(I am I). If you take off the blinkers, you will see a fuller picture emerging. (I am I).

People search for the meaning of life. They look to the planets and the stars but they don't recognise what's under their nose. Yet it's good to know what's happening in space, to understand a little more of the live physical process we are part of. But the garden we were given – that we birthed to explore and to rescue, to undo things we too did to it – is suffering and falling apart. We've damaged the oceans as well as the land. We war with ourselves and each other. The meaning of life is not out in space – it's within as we work to know our true selves and potential.

If I'm alive – and really I am – then to all intents and purposes, as far as life physical, I exist without form. This in itself has massive potential because it also can mean that life does exist on other planets, that we ourselves simply can't see it with physical eyes or equipment. But hasn't that knowledge been there all along? We just didn't compute it correctly.

> (I am I). At the start when life stirred – it too had no form. Without form or knowing – it wondered what it was. That same stirring exists inside people, whether in form or without. It's the very same dialogue that occurs in every person every day. What else did you think you spoke to with your millions of ongoing thoughts? (I am I).

CHAPTER 24

(I am I). Beautiful times are the result of a good life lived in tune with creation at its best. Everyone has control of their own will. Every will must become something bigger. Life has no choice but to follow, as it has no will of its own. I try to assist where I can, but that assistance relies on requests in the first place. Because of free will – My will allows each soul free rein. Karma, attraction, cause and effect ensure that what occurs is in tune with instructions then possible. (I am I).

Behind your actions are thoughts and intent. Intent is the signal that first powers thought, which then culminates into action. Action is already the effect, not the cause, although action becomes cause when it sets off other actions – like ripple effects upon water. All things become both the cause and effect at different times. How often have we put working faith into projects and people that could not/did not deliver on promise?

Earth will find a way to let you know what you need to know – but you must be receptive to its language.

Every soul has a built-in survival need to improve itself, to become more than its birth limitations, but instead of understanding and working with this, many work to dominate life and others. They want to be the leader – or for some to be the followers of others who appear to do better. The purpose of life is to work these things out of the system, your system, to then see if *Heaven* exists anywhere for you – Heaven being the bliss, contentment, love, peace and happiness searched for. When what you want is obtained, it's often not what you thought it would be. Victory, once over, leaves one empty; the soul then looks for the next fix it can reach for and so the whole process continues.

In an entire lifetime lived, it's possible to never really find your own version of 'happy'.

Body can only relate to matters physical. Ego is strong. It keeps kicking in to keep you safe, safe within boundaries you set long ago before the time you'd know better. Ego feeds emotions. Emotions become feelings. Feelings add to thought which produces more emotions. But which represents the real you? How would you know unless you've sat down alone to work this out? Again you can only work within the parameters of what you know already – but even then, that may not be the truth. You know what you've been fed – thought, shown, heard, learned and picked up along the way. This you then put together yourself to build up a picture, a representation of how you believe/believed life to be. Not all was true. Much was passed down as beliefs or half-truths of others, of hearsay or of what they were told in their own time.

So, how does all this affect Heaven?

All you've lived and held closely as truths become your beliefs. Beliefs knit together to become your core ethics. This ethos directly affected how you then lived and acted. All together this became who you were and the foundations of how you travelled through life. A whole lifetime lived is the legacy you feed into life – which becomes the sum total of what you'll take with you.

(I am I). Soul is the place where all this is stored, not for storage's sake but for growth,

for reasons of further/future attainment. How do you think people birth into the varied levels of physical life that exist? Nothing is accidental. Life has no favourites. Very little is as it would appear on the surface. Life IS change and growth – nothing remains static. How would life evolve if it did that? (I am I).

Because we accept our beliefs and we become what we believe (within the parameters of what can be achieved), when we feel hurt or if life doesn't respond in ways we expect, we take all that happens too personally. I was a prime example. I put far too much pressure on myself. Pressure then led me to worry and stress. To let go of stress, I learned to play even harder because on some level I felt I deserved to let go as my payment and a way to switch off, to compensate for what I thought was my worth.

But this can be a game full of danger that we accept, adapt to and make up as we go along, with ourselves as the main star, the central lead character – or victim.

(I am I). If most of your story plays out inside your own mind – how will anyone understand or ever know what you need to feel loved and secure? How can you ever even find these things yourself if you never

step back and look in? No one will know the true you until you know yourself better that way first. (I am I).

Your soul holds the record of all lives and activities that you have previously been through. It also knows why you chose what you are living. It knows what must be gained from all karma you have to move through. Karma is not there for you to get stuck in. Instead, it exists as that which you must overcome and move through. Nothing occurs that you can't handle. You're resourceful, ingenious, unique... The storyline you have lived, you chose yourself – but for now you just might not know why....

Every person is different. All have different joys, highs and lows playing out. Belief in your joy is the same as belief in your fear. It's the same working process. The same energy. It carries the same clout and force. The key is to recognise which vibration you are on.

CHAPTER 25

(I am I). Heaven...

Every person upon Earth will have their own ideas of what it's like and what it means to them to now have life here.

Heaven works the same, with different levels and different areas for different live experiences and expressions to continue. All areas co-exist as one – but all are individual, just as different countries upon Earth's crust differ also. This by no means undermines the importance of each section, but instead it gives you some example of how the whole thing operates to house many varied levels of those alive.

Within Earth's solar system, it's clearly visible that Earth is different from any other planet near or far. Earth houses physical life. It is completely self-contained by conscious mind. Every life force within its own sphere is alive because of it. Nothing could exist in physical form in other places that are born from it – unless exact conditions to support form are replicated, but only whilst in body. When the body falls away, all this will change.

Energy of the planet will not just poof away. It moves between neutrality, between having form and being formless at different times. This energy is life – it's raw creation/ cosmic conscious life in its purest form. Of itself to humankind it would be undefinable, only becoming recognised as being present when it takes on shapes and identity. But don't mistake its presence as being separate or divisible. All such shapes are aspects of itself – regardless of how each looks, works or acts – as one totality, one conscious working body that together we know as life, just as your own internal organs can be seen as individual, but when viewed from body's exterior perspective, all work as one.

Every lifeform/person on the planet will birth and die, arrive and depart, many times. Very few have only one life, unless they are unique and highly evolved already as God-realised conscious souls. All were non-existent physically until one conscious sperm reached one fertile egg to produce cell duplication to form matter. Not all forms come to birth in this way – but in general terms today, that's the consensus.

Before life was ever physical, conscious energy still existed without form. It had no form, knew nothing about form, was neutral, raw, unwritten, uneducated, without labels or identity, aim or purpose. It was blank. It had no past or future and knew nothing about NOW – about itself.

People are the ones who give to life its meaning. Every generation adds more to those before and so life learns, adapts, continues.

Memory works as individual portions of conscious mind. Each soul is individual, existing as itself as though disconnected and self-contained. But the nature of live *energy means it cannot be contained. It's everywhere, in everything, enveloping the whole planet. It was before – it still is now – and will be until the end – but there is no end. Energy is life and life by is very nature is eternal.*

Life itself within physical form is just a passing phase. It's all one single chapter in the existence of what is NOW – but NOW is never ending. All time past was NOW time once. All future will at some point become NOW until that time has passed. NOW is the only moment in reality that exists.

When a soul is born – it leaves the place of no form (or form of form much finer) where it lived until that moment – to become form within a body – made especially for the purpose to grant it a physical cloak/shell/ vehicle – to enable it to know this physical life. To express/experience/understand and know life in every way it is able is the purpose. When that time is over, soul again vacates the body and journeys (gravitates/ floats/instantly appears) back home, back to a level without form to all senses of physical body – but not to soul. (I am I).

CHAPTER 26

(I am I). When you dream, you operate as
though alive and physical – but you are fast
asleep and unmoving... Dream-state is the
closest thing that can compare to Heaven/
the afterlife. All you can imagine or dreams
can invent is able to occur. Every night your
conscious mind roams freely. Rest and sleep
are only needed by the body. Mind requires
change and stimulation. It cannot rest. The
closest thing to rest for mind is meditation,
the act of coming back to peace, to
no-thought, calm, tranquillity, to let go of
present dramas/scripts and become still.

When mind/soul is without form, no boundaries exist to hold it back or to keep it bound in check. It's free to roam to where its pleasures are, towards the places it feels most at home. It goes to where its frequency fits best. Remember that like attracts like. What's the same collects together to create a larger mass, as the natural laws of physics will also show.

When a life is over, each soul will still feel much the same as when it was alive physically. In life you have a body, but you don't think in terms of body, you just are... When body falls away, you still will feel the same. You still will be the same self as you were. You'll still be you.

Heaven is a label given to identify the place that you'll return to once your life physical is through. But it's also the same place that each living soul comes from when it's about to birth into a body specifically grown for that use.

Every soul comes from this place without exception. Every soul will be invited by the energy of acts of love of its parents at its conception.

How you live your life and how you process data is unique and up to you – but at no time are you disconnected from life's own bigger picture. At no time are you left abandoned to fend alone. To believe so is a myth handed down by generations, until true communication appears itself to be unusual or most odd instead of natural.

How could the live energy of life disconnect or separate from itself when in reality each living soul exists and lives within those very energies themselves? To do so would be impossible.

Heaven is the place you came from. It is to there you will return when your time is over in physical form, when this present chapter is all through. Physical form/body will not be necessary. In the same way as you now do in sleep, you'll continue on with life – in energy form.

Every life is individual. Each is here on Earth for their own specific reasons. Each will use their time and energy and then return again from whence they came when that time has passed.

It used to be enough to walk this physical journey as if blinkered or asleep, not knowing more existed until that life was through. But human input into life is rearranging the basic structure. Truths must now be clearer to grant a better understanding of the broader picture all feed into. The idea of separation is an untruth. Everything is joined. All thoughts and actions manifest into denser matter. Instead of thinking you're at the mercy of what might occur or come along, understand that you attract it (for personal reasons). You are the instigator of what you want/don't want, of what you need, desire and yearn for in some way to experience, express and then further to explore. Behind all your deepest thoughts, life itself is listening and responding without discernment/prejudice. Every lifetime though much the same, has purpose running in the background to give it a greater chance to reach intended goals within its time here.

Every soul must be allowed to create its personal kingdom while on Earth. Each must use free will and choice to discover what life and living really means within time now. Each aims personally to become more than it was before, so each soul then chooses its limitations and baseline gifts to be explored, fine-tuned, understood or superseded as deemed appropriate, along with karma underlining the whole thing.

Every lifetime will take you where your soul most needs to go – unless you fall, stumble, get stuck or lost along the way.

Many people understand more about these things now than ever before, but many more are still sleepwalking their way through their physical life, unaware or unconcerned of the wider implications of daily actions. (I am I).

No one had explained these things to me like this before. Ancient texts are not plain talking. Instead they speak in riddles or old language that needs deciphering. Deciphering leads to what you read into the words yourself depending on intelligence, need or mind-set. Past teachings prefer to dictate how to live or be – instead of teaching independent understanding and creativity. I had personally rebelled against exactly this. I was living more existence than real freedom and the rights I had to keep exploring.

Why are we often like that? I had been searching for the answers to my own deep probing questions. Why are we as we are? Why do we live the way we do? What keeps us moving in specific circles? How, when we have freedom, are we trapped?

Often even when we think we're free we're still not because we've placed restrictions on ourselves. How can we understand what we do not?

Heaven is not a prize. It's where we go when life is through, when our personal physical journey and lifetime works are over. I had lived a full life, richer in many ways than most, but still I hadn't grasped its much wider implications. Instead I had to die to understand this.

Books were not my thing. I like to talk to people to chat and hear experiences, their personal stories, first-hand. I was a good storyteller myself, much to the entertainment of friends and family. I was active but more into my music, my computer, technology of every kind, riding my push-bike and general TV/ science fiction/documentaries. Early youth had been my playground with cars, boats, motorbikes, wet-bikes/jet-skis/go-karts, in fact anything that had an engine was my pleasure. But nothing quelled my thirst. I didn't know what I needed or that something was missing. A subconscious battle was occurring deep within me.

Everything I chose to do or to be eventually became a chore or lost its sparkle. Nothing really was as I'd expected. In reality I'd been searching to find my place in life for my whole life, but regardless of how privileged I was, how many things I tried, I couldn't find it – but not for any reason I could name.

My home, where I am now, is very basic. Anything I want or need it's possible for me to have – but because I had so much while I was still on Earth,

I've come to realise that I need little. Here attention is better placed on other things.

We have homes/houses and we work. We still can eat and drink – but we don't *need* it. We don't need cars to travel but we can have them if we want them for enjoyment. Technology still exists but it's indescribably more advanced – not so dense and clumpy. Most new inventions upon Earth are good ideas that filter through from here to receptive minds, as the next step in new development and learning. Clothes and fashion still exist but are not held in such high regard – on my level here at least. I think in other places this may differ. I have been informed that when we come to Heaven, those who had harsh lives still want to explore their personal happiness in terms of what they feel they missed out on or lacked. For those souls, these things then happen. Every individual gets to fulfil their fantasy or unexplored, unrecognised and unfinished goals to discover if true happiness, love, bliss or greater peace for them exists there.

Love is the overriding factor here. Everyone comes to the level most in tune with their energy signature. This means where you end up hopefully will make you happy. This is the reason we came to Earth to birth in the first place, to allow us to fine-tune our vibrations through the life we freely chose and lived, ending in our return to spiritual levels much improved.

Much explained so far still relates more to the physical. But it still doesn't adequately explain the why: why we need to know this stuff; why I'm writing this book with my wife instead of being on a jolly or doing something else; why we yo-yo back and forth so often between life in physical form and Heaven; why it's so important to understand that life continues; why we need to know the full price of our actions...

CHAPTER 27

Before birth we live in the realms of spirit, there's every chance that we've been on Earth before in a different time frame. During that time, we lived life largely as we do now by feeling, intuiting, thinking, being taught, forced, lead or not as we went through it. Lives were long or short and then we *died*. Every time we die, we end up here – back at where we came from in the first place. If you cast your mind back, even just a bit through recent history, you can see how you've evolved to reach this point. Every life has been in search of self-fulfilment, survival, love, peace, development, happiness, riches, bliss etc, even during this one. These things have been the single driving factors that have kept us going and evolving.

How many times we have lived and died and lived and died who can tell, it's not important, but what is important now is where you've reached. This life you currently own is the most important life you've had so far. It sets the precedent for what will happen next time round.

Have you never wondered why some folk have so much and others so very little? Each soul is on their own place on their ladder of improvement, wisdom gathering and higher understanding/exploration/ learning. Very little is how it first looks on the surface.

In Heaven, when you get here, the first gain is whether or not you can go forward into the levels of your choosing from before the time you last birthed. The second gain is whether you can remain in Heaven – or whether you need to come back fairly quickly to put things straight or try again. Remember, very few souls will freely choose the darker realms as their new residence. But even choosing is a gift – it's *a gift* if you are able to even do that. The darker the soul – the darker the level they return back into when they get here. Not all will get the chance to come straight back.

On Earth we're now exploring, remembering, rediscovering this information. In the afterlife these things are obvious. We sometimes choose to birth to *try to wake up quickly out of sleep*, to help ourselves and one another *get back home*.

(I am I). Before the original first sin – Heaven was fully present on physical Earth. But over millennia and generations being born – this connection was reported to be lost. Subsequently feeling separate and alone, negativity spread through lower base/barbaric actions. Humans would do everything they did just to survive. But as knowledge of life eternal faded, diluted or was lost, people thought they had only one life. Feeling self-contained, they thought whatever was kept unseen really could be hidden. The shock that each soul then felt upon their own return to spirit after physical death is just the same for each that is felt now.

No one snuffs right out or becomes extinguished upon physical death. All souls continue on and take with them the lifelong gifts, baggage and unfinished business this lifetime accrued.

I am real. I'm not pretend. Open up to the possibility and feel the difference this will make to you and to your life. What do you have to lose? If you don't try you'll never know. But don't wait until your life is over to find out.

To live a half life when a full life is available is a shame. It would mean you must repeat much of the same again to reach this point. Do you want that? You can have that if you want to, but today, unlike in the past, it's not always strictly necessary. All options are available for you to go through and explore for truth's validity.

Don't throw caution to the wind – progress steadily, even slowly, but progress – this is important. Every time a life is over, your present book is firmly closed. You'll have to wait in line for the next slot to return – but only when the exact conditions are available to make it right to aid and help you – and when conditions left in this life have played out to their full extent through other people and events you left unfolding.

Nothing is too difficult that you can't overcome it. Where you are is where you should be to take the next presenting steps. Begin to notice where your life feels stuck. Find the reasons why. Go inside yourself to find the deeper cause and readjust. Nothing in life from life-outside can reach that inner spot. (For deeper understanding about these

*things – and more – read And So It Begins...,
Believe & Achieve, Life Is Calling..., Divine
Guidance and the workshops on our website
for personal use at home.)*

*Everything you do on Earth affects your
time in Heaven. This is not about being
good, that's not the issue here, but more
about your own connection, your life force/
energy signature. This is what you bring to
life's own table, what you receive, feed out,
give back; this is your live creative link, your
own instructions into life's real-time living
matrix. I respond according to those
directives you give out. How else could free
will work? How else could you attract? How
else could you connect and life respond,
deliver? (I am I).*

This is my book. I am writing this to help others
wake up to truths around them. This is not about
religion – your own beliefs and inherent chosen
paths are personal free will and choice. This is more
about the inner workings of yourself, what you are
really part of, how you connect to life, how it
responds and what will happen to you once your
allotted time on Earth has passed and for you this
life is through.

To move forward myself, I had to do this or I too
would be responsible for things in life I'd thwarted

as untrue, impossible, out of my jurisdiction or current interest.

Friends, family, loved ones, strangers and even children die, sometimes out of order or seemingly out of sync – but they don't disappear. They come to see you, spend time with you, join in with love and fun… They still exist. Their lives continue. They try to let you know when they are around to bring you comfort, to ease your pain, to bring you love and to say thank you for loving/knowing/caring, being there for them…They remain a living part of the journey you're still on – just mainly unseen.

But why? Why do they and even I, keep trying hard to prove this? Don't imagine they don't have better ways to fill their time. So why do we try so hard to prove we are around, that we know what's going on with you and wider family/friends/issues and society…?

People are now beginning to accept this. But few again look deeper to understand the why: why we're trying hard to prove that life continues, that we exist, that death is an illusion, that it doesn't actually exist in quite the way you think… Death is just a temporary transition, the discarding/falling away of body – like a cloak removal. Life continues – so do we. As I did too.

(I am I). Everything you are continues with you. All you've been, done and become,

your weaknesses, flaws and strengths, will carry on unless they're overcome or no longer relevant. Some were just to help you within this single lifetime, to hold you up and keep you strong or as things to overcome to help you grow/evolve. That's the reason that this book is so important.

Waking up to higher truths will not turn you into something you are not. This is not about religion, not about being a hippy or a need to go and hug some trees (although you can if you feel so inclined and it fulfils and makes you happy). This is more about awakening and awareness, about recognition and remembrance of the self. You are a powerful creator in your own right. I am part of you – so you too connect to Me. It's important you understand how you use/abuse/misinterpret your connection. It's not good enough to live and think we'll see..., that at some point later if this shift is true I will find out... You can choose this if you like, but in the meantime you'll live how now? What else will you rack up in baggage/karma?

Regardless of the past – draw a line. Step over, readjust, learn, search, explore in any way you can to gain the answers to the questions you are gathering. Don't get sad, mad, depressed or cross. Let go of personal, public judgement. This is not the time to climb on your high horse.

Don't look at others and believe that you have wronged them – and they you. Let these things go, not because they are not true – but because with understanding, you'll view the whole thing differently later on. No big moves or jumps. Tread water. Stay exactly where you are, do what you must do, honour your commitments and essentials. Disconnect for now from what you view as problems on personal levels, not to just ignore them or to pretend they don't exist – but because again you'll view them differently as life unfolds a little further. This is not the same as shirking responsibilities. Be all you should be to all parties. Play the role you must – for that's your personal contribution into life. Keep all things turning, flowing, correctly balanced as they should be.

*Waking up is not a chore. It is a gift. It's a gift that you have earned and are more than ready for. It's the reason that your life has been the way it has already, though you don't realise – you're so much more…
(I am I).*

CHAPTER 28

I had to die to learn this stuff because I was too stubborn to admit I could see there was truth in what my wife was saying. When you wait too long, it's not easy to do a u-turn and keep face. Pride gets in the way, especially when you've said things and acted harshly to the contrary – even with hostility – for a long time.

This stuff is big. It reaches in and touches places you've never looked at or felt before or feel unsure/insecure/uncomfortable about. No one is saying you are not good enough, that efforts given weren't enough or that you're wrong in personal character and outlook. This is not a dig at you. I thought my *self and purpose* were being questioned, judged, but that was not the case. I was proud and stubborn. I held tightly onto what I'd lived, worked out and toiled a lifetime so far to achieve and reach. In essence, I was too stubborn to admit there might be more – because I'd missed it. *Me – I'd missed it.* I was *the* person that was streetwise, the person who missed nothing on any level, the one that others came to when they had any problem – I helped them out... So to swallow that I had missed something as big as this – that was too bitter to acknowledge or back down from. It hurt. I was hurt. I was hurting that my wife needed more when I'd given and freely shared all I had. On base level now, as I look back, I can see that I no longer felt of value.

I wish I had taken the time to investigate this further. It's not new. Huge amounts of people have written lots about this topic on many levels, each trying to convey/explain it in their own way to reach those on their specific wavelengths of belief or thinking. Even the music that I'd listened to for hours contained this same information – but unless you are aware or thinking on those levels – you still won't hear it. We process everything from the levels of understanding we are at.

Huge value is placed on building up a life and lifestyle and then keeping it at that level of achievement. But that's not really how life is supposed to be entirely. You are not your things

– regardless of how impressive, big and beautiful they are. You are not your chosen/attained profession – for that's just what you do or where so far you've reached. All these things and more, apart from gains and obvious physical value, are outwardly projections – labels you have learned to wear to judge the world – or how it judges you.

In my own life I came through stages of having very little. Because of this I vowed life would be better – and it was. But then I worked hard to protect and to sustain it, to keep up with technology and life's many changes. I had the best. But nothing that you own can make you happy. That's just survival and a quality of life you can enjoy, a short fix. This is no problem unless you have everything and you're bored, you've lost your true life spark, you find there's not much left, that life is empty, that where you are does not fulfil you as you thought it would... This used to be labelled 'the mid-life/ middle age crisis'.

I tried to recapture and hold tight to what I'd valued in my youth, what I thought I'd lost or was lacking with the youth I saw today. I rebelled against expectations and stereotypes. I was not equipped to get old quietly, gracefully. I'd be the best, most hip younger-older style person I could be. And it worked. Surrounded with my friends and my children's younger ones, I'd had time on my hands to find the fun.

That's where I was within myself the night I'd passed. Happy but yet not... Argumentative (because it was my right and I'd enjoyed a good old moan. My wife called me a cross between Victor Meldrew and Alf Garnett – fictional TV characters played by actors Richard Wilson and Warren Mitchell). I went to bed as I'd always done a thousand times before – then I was dreaming... I tried to wake up – but I died instead.

I had to go. My body broke down. There was no way then that I could stay.

If I'd have known about all of this earlier – would my life have been better? It would have been different because I'd have understood it all better. I'd have taken better care of myself, not to the point that many people do now – that stuff was never for me. I didn't need to be the best looking, fittest, most pumped up person around – although I was competitive. Didn't use Botox, didn't use steroids, didn't see the need to be fanatical about diet, fashion or designer labels – but had enjoyed the best in other ways. I'd relish a good meal, even really loved food, enjoyed feeling and being alive, loved the sea, loved home comforts and friends. My family was the best – even though they drove me mad and I them too. I can't say my life would have been better – just different. It would have made better sense. I would not have felt redundant but instead full of purpose, life zest and peace...

To have known about this would have helped me leave more in my wake – in the form of contribution and make more of a difference to life – not in a do-gooder fashion, but something more purposeful with meaning, to change some of the rubbish that had made me mad instead. My wife used to say that I should use my voice – not to shout – but to put more wrong things right. (I was very opinionated and opposed to much I thought wrong, forgotten or overlooked. I hated with a passion to see others bullied, used or abused. I'd seen too much of that in early youth first-hand myself.)

From where I am now, I can see these things gave me strengths I didn't recognise, unique perspectives and insights. I'd held them inside as hurts and negatives instead of using them as rungs to climb up higher.

The books my own wife had written could have helped me – but stubbornness and pride instead had held me back. So much hurt could have easily been avoided...

> (I am I). Having answers to deep questions you don't always know you carry takes the heavy toil and worry out of living. You still must put what's needed in place to keep things in order, but life itself will then step

up to help. Not all you're going through were you supposed to; not everything you carry is strictly yours; not all should weigh so heavily or stay longer than strictly necessary; most of your karma is over and life itself is waiting for fresh directions. (I am I).

CHAPTER 29

We came to birth to live a whole life of our own creativity and choosing, but along with that we also came here to wake up. Only when living on Earth can changes that we make become permanent. Only on Earth can you evolve further and change your vibration, your life force. This is the aim – not the struggle to survive at any cost, to accumulate, grow old and then vacate…

I was not ready to go but in the end I had no choice.

Now I understand. Life's picture is bigger than you think. You can't always recognise the role that you play or know why you do. But nothing is hidden.

All things are known. Everyone and everything connects.

> *(I am I). I will not let anyone fail. That's why many will re-birth so quickly – to try again, again and again to achieve whatever it is they said they would – in ways that with their knowledge and outlook only they are able. These things are not chores – but privileged gifts. It's a gift to help a life or to make a difference – a difference that may be followed for hundreds of years to come – assisting others to find their own light or their chosen path... (I am I).*

I watch my family now and there is nothing I can do to make life easier. We think of time as linear, as a lifetime stretching ahead, as it being a long time – but it's not. Not everyone gets a tomorrow. Much thought is projected into a possible, expected or make believe future, but today is where all things occur, it's the place that all things stem from. I was taught to be disciplined at a time in youth when in truth I had very little; it stood me in good stead and really helped me. Later I was self-disciplined enough to keep my personal paperwork, accounts and work completely up-to-date. Daily chores were always completed. My physical contributions couldn't be faulted – and to be honest – I was always proud of that. I'd planned for old age but the economy and the government kept moving expected goal posts further back. I didn't see I would never reach that place myself...

In itself, that wasn't the issue. What was more problematic was that I hadn't ever considered soul and what that word really meant. To live a whole life on the planet and to not really move further forward is a shame. Again, that's why I'm writing this book now. Maybe I went a bit too early, maybe I didn't – but if I hadn't, you yourself would not be reading this – so who can judge?

My journey is not over. Instead it's starting again. There's so much to do and to enjoy here – but only for those whose lifetime expectancy was pretty much naturally through (excluding unforeseen illness, accidents or worse...). If you take your life too early by your own free will and actions, then you come into a place of understanding, learning and adjustment. You do find peace. It's not easy to watch those you love – and who loved you – really hurting. They carry the memory and effects of what occurred around with them, physically, for the rest of their natural lives. You'll realise the depth of this when you see the bigger picture, finally understanding that not everything revolved around yourself – even though in many ways it did, and that's the old catch-22 in play again.

Work exists on Earth to keep life going and to grant you ways to gain the money to help you live. Some do it mainly to give life something back... Over here the same occurs, but the reason we work is always and only to be of service. Currency is not required.

Heaven is a continuation of life itself – only better. This is not to say that life on Earth is worse, but it sure is harder. Negative thinking and behaviour make things worse. Until the current traumas have been worked through, happiness for all will be but fleeting – unless you can control that and hold life's own energy steady...

Again that's why I'm writing this book: to allow it to be seen that much of what is carried daily is pretend, pointless and not worth the effort and worry it takes. Life is too short. It's really precious. You don't know the day you won't wake up – or again the day you'll never sleep – through an unfortunate incident... When you reach these levels here you'll see things differently – but then you won't be present physically to do anything more about it...I am luckier than most. Who do *you* know on Earth who *would realise* if you were around – let alone pick up and finish what your soul had still left to accomplish?

No one but you can know and carry the millions of thoughts that you think. Every person has their own internal dialogue going on. But to whom and to what do we speak? No one knows this better than you; but it's such a fundamental, integrated part that you probably didn't consciously recognise it even happens.

Every thought that fed belief or led to action is recorded – not only your own – but for everyone. That's part of the replay playing back to you after death. Nothing is missed. I myself have been through it already...

Much truth and illusion exists in this ongoing dialogue. It's this and this alone that's responsible for what plays out in life. The problem is that no one else can hear it (except God/Life/Source/the Universal Oneness) so no one else can tell you if you're wrong. What you believe remains with you until at some point it may be highlighted physically through action – word – intent – mistake. More occurs inside yourself than you'll ever let anyone see; no wonder you can feel misunderstood. But so too does nearly everyone else... All try to make themselves understood, to live a good life, to find happiness, love and personal creature comforts – all are searching to find the same things to make them feel complete.

In life we aim to evolve, to better ourself in ways we think that we can. We look for enjoyment and whatever fruits our chosen life path will bring along. When we die, whether from old age, sickness or accidental death, all that we've amassed is left behind. We're as naked in many ways as when we birthed. So there has to be a deeper meaning to this live ongoing struggle.

Much hope is placed on religion. But religion is not the means – just a signpost, each presenting itself as if *only their way is right* – which means they're actually saying all others are wrong. But that's *not* so. All are wrong just as much as they all do have some things right. They are only a way, one way, one single pathway up the side of a very high mountain. That's all. If you knew nothing about religion, if that was the only way to get back home and you knew nothing of it, then you'd be stuffed. But it's not. All answers that you search for are already embedded in you. That's why, in many ways, you might rebel. You are the door, the lock and even the key to your own future. You are in charge. But just like an expedition to the top of Mountain Everest – don't set your sights on the peak alone – or you'll never get back. The objective is to get there *and* back. Life is the same. Don't focus just on time spent here alone. Begin to acknowledge there's more – a lot more – notice things – information, signs and signals around you that pop up and then adjust.

Life responds to you. It works alongside you in unison every day.

> (I am I). *Many levels exist here in Heaven that explain even more of this shift. Not all souls in Heaven reach even this much awareness – just as on Earth, it's the same. You are reading this book. That alone is priceless and places you ahead of the game. You can't un-know what you have*

learned – so life has no choice but to react and to then respond, but with this knowledge comes responsibility, responsibility to live your life right, not as a god, a saint or a guru – but to learn and understand what your connection to this life and you yourself are part of – not only for now but for always.

I have waited a long time for you to reach this point. You too have birthed and died many times to also reach this place. The fact you're still alive today means you have more work to do, more items on your soul agenda to check out. Don't fall at the fence, keep on going. I will uphold you. The hardest part is over – you're now through to the next stage of your journey.

I am real. You are real. The dialogue we share together is real also. Instructions you send out to life – whether you realise you do, have done or not – are also as real within real time as you can get. (I am I).

CHAPTER 30

(I am I). Every person has their own direct link to the planet, to larger life, to Me. Without this link, you would not even have life. Physical life would not exist anywhere at all without it – for I AM LIFE. Fear and hate, worry and depression, jealousy, retaliation, stress, injustice and much more run counter-productive to all of this and will knock your link off balance. Believe in them long enough and you'll feel yourself alone – although you're not. You'll simply be on a slightly different wavelength. When you're on a different wavelength, how can you receive what's waiting to come in as rightfully yours from life on purer levels?

How can you reach life's own live real-time assistance that's yours by birthright, that in all truth you link into as a working, conscious entity and live channel... How can life provide you with what you need if you don't even ask – let alone believe this link exists?

Of its own accord, life will not decide or know when something is good or bad for you. It knows nothing of good or bad; it has no choice, discernment and cannot argue – knowing only what now is. Instead these traits were given straight to people to use themselves, to learn, grow and explore, to make choices and decisions appropriate. That's the potency and power that each person wields, the gifts each one fine-tunes to use at will.

In Heaven, as on Earth, each person has the task of finding love and happiness, bliss, joy, peace and the place in life's own thriving matrix where they best fit. Everyone has the same chance to evolve, to climb higher and ever higher towards their life goals and their own sense of nirvana. I AM the living consciousness, the totality of everything. I am pure love without duality. Duality was made by humans. The first sin long ago was the original first split. Not really an actual split, but more through negative thought a separation, a temporary fall into illusion. But like any loving parent, would I then just disappear through a mistake (which has led to many more mistakes)? Would I walk away? Could I disconnect from any single part of my own self? Could you disengage from your own life force? I could not. You could not. To separate in this way would be impossible.

How often and in how very many more ways will I tell you – that you are love and loved, that you are important, that your happiness is also? Not just for Me, but for you too.

Each life you live becomes another chance for you to fine tune your soul energy, your real self, your understanding and achievements to a new vibration. Only while on Earth in physical form can this be done and kept long term. What you are, you become – and you own.

Each lifetime you possess becomes the single most important one you've ever lived because it resonates and connects you personally to Now – because it is Now. Time has either been or is yet still to become now, for Now is in all reality the only timeframe that exists. Past and future belong to ether until they converge in Now's reality. Now is the creative time-place of life's own focus; it's where aspects of everything converge and the only point that I can ever be accessed.

Physically, nothing else exists. All else is energy without form until that's changed by life, by matter, nature, people, growth and evolution or all combined.

Life is energy, conscious energy. Energy cannot snuff out. It just is. It can shape, reshape and change its charge (positive – negative – neutral). Because it cannot disappear, it stays part of a working system, just as night becomes day becomes night for ever more in cycles or succession. As you become happier, your energy becomes lighter, finer and brighter... You'll attract more of the same because like attracts like. When you are happy, blissful, balanced or at peace/more content, my own life force is also fuelled because unconditionally we're connected through positivity. Your health and also My own receives the benefit.

For the best to occur, you must become aware of what you're thinking, believing, enacting, responding to and expecting. You have time to improve – before your storyline is over, to fine-tune and adjust, to explore your own gifts and potential. Move beyond the space of living for survival's sake alone because when you work on higher levels, those most basic needs will be met, even if you do so in the last minute yourself. Shift your point of focus onto what drops into your awareness and what you can add – to make things work better for you and for life's unfolding picture. Remember you are the thinking, working and actioning point of real-time life, of Now. What's achieved you'll keep for always which in turn propels you lower/higher to shape/attract more going forward.

Birth is just the entry of one soul into the density of this physical level. Death is rebirth or re-entry of that same soul back to its natural home. During the whole of its physical life, each soul is a vessel, a channel for Earth's own vibrant life force to flow through as it lives, enjoys and creates its own version of real-time life, continuously evolving and so growing. Each soul/vessel has the capacity to be as positive, vibrant, bright as it allows... Of course, through every life, negatives and positives do occur which then affect that soul's capacity to hold onto its true vibration; like a battery or a light, its brightness, power and even health will dip, change, diminish or increase as time unfolds. At the end of each life, what is left becomes the vibration/energy signature you take with you going forward. Not only that, all through life you continuously feed that same live energy and drive that you're producing back to Earth. You top up/diminish/help or detract from life's own reservoir of resources as your personal contribution – deliberate or not. Because of this, you become responsible for what occurs within your story and the larger world events unfolding on life's stage.

Remember, like attracts like to create more of the same. Enough sameness added together then becomes a mass. Mass adds to mass to become an even greater mass which adds strength and power to beliefs, to behaviour patterns and existing trends as more join in. Therefore, far from being the victim of what in Now occurs, you have the power/insight to navigate and to control it.

Much is the way it is in life because fear is the underlying driving factor behind what occurs instead of love. Not 'flower power' love but understanding, unconditional love and trust; not blind trust that goes against the grain of good sense and obvious truth, but trust and inner knowing that when you allow it, life will always work in unison along with you to help the best that can be to come in.

Life is your gift, not your punishment or chore. You chose to be here for another allotted time span, but time is that which is most overlooked. Your time and life force are very precious; like sand can't help but run inside the workings of an egg-timer, both time and life force have no choice but to drain away...

When life becomes most difficult, that usually indicates a shift of some kind coming in. Don't get depressed, sad, worried, scared, drained or down; instead find the most obvious solution, the bottom line of truth between what has happened and what needs then to come in next and go with it. Most choices are just for now, a stepping stone to something else perhaps not yet available or in view. Trust. Go with it. See where the pathway/options lead. Life will support you better when you remove all doubt and fear you carry.

An entire shift of consciousness is birthing through. This is natural and will touch every life. It's Earth itself evolving as intelligence, understanding and needs then shift. Remember – life has little choice but to give, respond. You are affected also, not as punishment or chore – but as a gift, something you too birthed right now to witness and to add more to.

Every moment lived and breathed here is precious. Each person is very needed. Every point of view lived honestly adds structure and further meaning to what's unfolding. Even when you reach 100, you still will be important for you'll still have more to add, to wake up, shake up and make sense of what's occurring, to understand, accept, release and to overcome your attitude and personal memories of life's failings: all activities, triumphs, gifts and avenues explored, used, unused or missed... All aspects of everything must be finalised here to be of value and owned positively going forward or things unfinished may become future karma or soul contracts to be worked through/again repeated. (I am I)

Death is only a transition between each stage of life as a butterfly goes through the same, through metamorphosis between living as a grub and transforming into butterfly, the difference being that a butterfly's metamorphosis is physical, therefore seen...

Every soul born on Earth chose to be here, regardless of what it later thinks. Earth is the original Garden of Eden as depicted. It's the only place conscious life (energy) can support matter (physical), the only place that conditions are right, the only place it can know how life feels and what to all intents and purposes *life* means. Things will make better sense as life evolves further towards bliss, balance and greater peace. Peace is not boring. It's not everyone acting and being identical. It just means we'll live together more comfortably, understanding one another, honouring similarities as well as differences, more able to share the same space.

Much more exists to being in Heaven than can be shared in just a few words, but the emphasis for now is placed more on current behaviours and beliefs that hinder or sabotage daily life, not just greater life – but your own. You are valued exactly as you are. When you realise the main reasons you are where you are and what you can do overall to make this experience better for yourself and for everyone, you'll be pleased. Only you can achieve what you birthed intentionally to do within this lifetime. Why would you instead prefer to doubt this?

Life provides exactly what's needed for all but it requires direct, clear instructions; all parties must speak the same language and pull in the same live direction together as One wave – One life force – One thriving evolving, conscious body.

Most pain and hardship carried comes from stress, doubt, fear, anxiety and uncertainty. Just like any virus in existence, these things can only produce more of the same vibration as themselves. To break the cycle, you must return to inner clemency, pull back inside your own self to reassess, levitate and climb higher, to see beyond what was said or is thought to be occurring, to find balance, truth and solutions. Let go of ego, of thoughts of being hurt/ offended... Let things like these pass, blow over and dig deeper, to find what within your heart your own soul knows.

CHAPTER 31

Not everything in life is good and great. Dangers exist, bad influences too.

(I am I). I am positive energy but negative also exists. All that's produced fits into one category of charge or the other. Negatives detract from life's health – whereas love, happiness and all things positive add more health and vitality to enhance it. Most souls on the planet are still working to perfect their own frequency definition. This task is not over until the very last breath has been taken.

Once life moves forward from that point, you can't change the place you've reached without returning back into body to complete yet another life cycle, unless what you've left behind is still playing out in response to what you set in motion. But then that's the danger. Not every soul will have another chance to return again as easily or as fast as they would like.

Some souls do not exit immediately or want to cross over at all to start their next chapter. For varied reasons at death they were not ready – some feel they have unfinished business or don't want to leave their loved ones behind – others are frightened, unsure of the reception that waits for them... Remember it is a shock, no matter who you are, to find that after death you are still living. For many, only then do they mentally review the life they have just lived and what through time spent here was so produced. (I am I).

I mostly knew decent people – but at times I did come into contact with others shadier. I wouldn't have liked to cross them or get into their bad books. I was friendly, respectful, civil – and they were too. We moved forward. But this world is full of many characters of varied types. Even within the company of villains, codes of conduct still apply. What they do in life they do for money, standing, respect, power, survival and sometimes in their own way even goodness, to keep their name and position in high regard within the leagues and circles they exist in. An eye for an eye is their motto. They've got to stay on top or someone else will come along and fight them for it. Once that way of life takes hold, it's not always an easy task to move beyond it. Someone's usually got a hidden trump card on you somewhere, just in case during a change of heart you might spill the beans on them ... Like a pack of dogs has its natural ranking order, so do the circles these people move in. Reputation means everything. Fear of being seen or known as less (becoming soft) is what drives them. Eat or be eaten...

So when these characters die, through murder or natural causes, again it can be tough to still exist beyond the point of death, especially when you've inhabited the darker shades of living while alive. Souls don't always change immediately when they die. These people here can be some who shy away from crossing over because they don't exactly know what to expect or what will greet them next – Hell or Heaven.

I hadn't been a bad man, not always strictly good, but not really that bad either and yet *I still had been left alone for many days beyond my time of passing.* I could have wandered anywhere and wreaked all kinds of havoc – but I was lucky, in the small amount of knowledge I somehow had I knew that I would be OK; though I didn't know why or where that *knowing* came from... People racked with anger, shame, hate, revenge, fear or guilt will find it even harder to locate their inner place of trust. For personal reasons, they'll be anxious, even scared of what will happen. Some instantly get whisked away...

> *(I am I). These are very good examples of how energy wavelength and vibration has altered from positive to negative. When a good soul dies, it gravitates straight through to Heaven, to the safety of those who care and so can help. I am positive. I have no option but to wait for lost souls to turn around and come back. I cannot override My own will that gave them free will. The danger for them is that they'll meet and join with others like-minded in the same predicament; equally rooted in negatives, to bolster one another and to continue the illusion of comradeship that they're living.*

> *These words are truth and not fiction. Whilst in body, duality exists as choices and decisions to keep things in order. The fight between good and bad, truth or otherwise,*

exists as morals, wants and needs that are chosen – but once body falls away, no such duality exists anymore – only the full force of the positive or negative vibration that's been gained within that lifetime.

There is no more duality. Nothing holds them back. Each soul becomes exactly what it made itself to be. Bad souls (for want of a better expression) feel the full force of their own fear and badness. Nothing will be able to change that unless realisation dawns and then they want change also. But the fear of what they've done or created can be stronger, as can revenge, hatred and more to keep things going. A negative does not contain light, for light and dark are opposites of the self-same sliding scale... So believing themselves alone, abandoned, lost, trapped or even on top of their game, souls can sometimes wander off or refuse to go forward. It's been known for some to exist for years – even tens or hundreds, wandering around alone or in a crowd, unaware they have only to trust or want to stop and turn these things around – even just a bit – for help to come. No scythe or grim reaper waits to catch and take them off to hell. No one else may see them; they themselves might meet no other soul either.

They'll continue as though they're still present to frequent the places and the people they knew or feel attached/ beholden to. Even those they hate. Nothing can restrict beliefs, behaviour or thoughts of anger, fear or doom they hold or feel. They live the version of the present they believe is real and valid; some are even unaware that they're now dead. (I am I).

Don't be mistaken: not every murdered victim hangs around within this state. Good souls go always straight back home, but for others, what they've done or have been through weighs heavily; what each soul must next do individually still plays its part. In reality, no one is alone – but not all souls immediately know this. So life itself has no alternative but to deliver what they believe, attract and ask for... Remember, life cannot overturn its own laws of free will and choice, cause, effect and attraction.

Some discarnate souls (those who have no body) gather close to people's energy (those still in body) they may have an interest in, with whom they feel some kind of affinity or with those that partake in activities that they too enjoyed while still here. We've discussed how when souls gather, a greater mass occurs which then adds to more enjoyment or distaste/disapproval to what's playing out... We've said also that through excessive use of alcohol and drugs, your own vibration quickly changes. You can feel that even for yourself while in the act.

There's a reason that when you drink, inhibitions fall away and you feel freer. You've switched your 'adult' off. A different side of self becomes pronounced, the side that might not be quite as capable of making good decisions that would normally keep you safe – or the side that feels it should hold more control. It's when you switch in this manner that other beings can come in closer to enjoy the moment/activities along with you. In essence, you've left your safety-gate wide open voluntarily. Don't we all know people who change completely when they drink? Don't we too? Or people who drink more and more and sometimes don't know how to stop, acting completely out of character and good conduct. It's not always just the substances themselves that makes them behave that way... It's possible to have many such attachments without knowing, like a crowd that walks along with you – but unseen. (Like people alive have gangs, groupies etc. that egg each other on.) These attachments bring you down, drain your energy resources ever lower and leave you feeling depressed, ill, depleted, angry, anxious, paranoid, unsafe, vulnerable or weak. Your character and outlook can change, you feel different but can't really put your finger on the reason why. Does this ring any bells – for self or others?

Therefore to protect yourself is really necessary, so that no one else (no other person/soul) can come too close to you without your angel's or your own higher self's consent. Sometimes these things may be allowed to continue for a while as means to reach a different end, for example, if through free will you're partaking too much in activities that smash your aura, or if you keep on letting go of your own good sense, if you're happy to vacate the premises of your body by remaining high or drunk excessively often. That's exactly what the saying means *that sometimes you have to hit rock bottom before you can start to come back up*, not as punishment but as a message to your senses/ awareness – to wake/shake you up to be different or to change. Remember you never know what you asked for on a higher soul level before you birthed. If you knew you'd have a problem, a hard habit to shift – you might have given permission for these things to occur to help you remember/ realise... Sometimes negatives occur to pull you back on track – like a stop sign.

No one else is allowed to walk inside your shoes and body except you, unless through actions of free will – voluntarily or not – you vacate your post and you then let them. Remember that you actually have an angel with you (belief is not an option because you can't personally change this) who will do their level best to keep you safe. But they can't override your own free will – or anyone else's who may sometimes get the upper hand. No one can. But even then, they will continue to aid and help, to make you see.

This is not said to make you paranoid – but to keep you safe. Nightclubs, casinos, public places, public transport hubs and any number of frequented public spaces are common areas for discarnate souls to live or linger or hang out. They may not intend possession but may come in close for other reasons, whether nosey because they like your energy, might want to share in what you're doing, may simply like the look of you, may be too stubborn or too scared to leave, or may be downright destructive because they don't like happy people and good energy. A million reasons could be applied as to why they feel attracted to people just like you. But if you keep protection up – not through paranoia – but just for safety's sake just in case, your angel can do the rest to protect you. You must however take at least one step by yourself by asking that you and your loved ones be kept safe…

The battle between light and darkness does exist – but not in terms or ways that you may think. The most you need to know right now is that positive energy helps your soul grow brighter, lighter, younger, stronger and more attractive, to attract more of what you want or need to ease your personal journey, to make you happier, healthier, feel more alive – more love, loved and loving… Earth then wins also because yours will be a channel that works correctly. Every real attempt to become a better person, no matter how seemingly insignificant or small, is met with instant real assistance on higher levels.

There are also yet other souls who really don't want this growth to happen. This links directly with energy vibration, with feeling comfortable or not. Negative souls can't feel comfortable when your energy is high or too strong or bright. You've maybe felt the same yourself when you've walked into rooms or places outside your own comfort zone. You prickle, feel uncomfortable and leave. That's the reason lesser souls don't want this shift to happen. They enjoy the place they're at and therefore have no desire to want to change it, even going out of their way to stop another when they see it coming and they're able. If these souls can't reach you, because you're protected, they sometimes try instead to reach friends, family and others close to cause disruption – in a bid to upset the status quo or to slow things right down with more obstacles. They'll use the person or people they can get the closest to through actions and activities and personal depressive mind sets – to make things turn…

That is what happened to me while I was still in body, although at the time I didn't know it. I allowed these individuals to come right in. It affected my personal outlook and then my state of health. I wouldn't have listened anyway had someone ever told me, but that's the reason I'm now sharing this information. These things are real. They're everywhere. Some were human once, and others, not. They drain your life-force, your sense of hope and plunge you deeper into sadness, self-loathing and depression. Then as you look around you'll blame everyone but yourself. But it's to *yourself* that you must look to find the answers – *and don't stop*. Don't look deeper for conspiracies, but truth. Be gentle with yourself, but firm and kind…

Remember these things happen out of view – you didn't even know before today they may exist – but now you do, and you do know how you daily feel. You know when you feel down or in despair but don't know why. The thing is not to panic but to keep your head. Even if you only wonder if this stuff is real or true – the smallest plea for help from you will bring protection and higher help directly through (from God/Source/the Universe and your personal angel). You'll feel empowered and protected – but don't stop there… Begin your own search to fuel your inner thirst for answers. Never feel embarrassed – because that's another negative that will hinder. No one holds a score card. Trust that you'll be guided, protected and held safe. The first step once again is just to want this.

To hold belief in unicorns and fairies is not needed here – unless you want to. To be scared that you might change or then be seen as weird is also not constructive. What do you have to lose by exploring or being open to the possibility these things are real and could be correct? Who but you knows what you feel or think (apart from life itself, as you're now learning)? What would be the benefit if you could find and keep more inner peace, if blood pressure and stress levels could be lowered quite dramatically without medication or external help, if mood swings between up and down could be lessened...? What if you could sleep at night and then wake up more refreshed, if you could really see the benefit of all you've lived, known and been through, if you could see clearer the opportunities around you now or coming up and in what direction, if any, you are heading? What if you could give family/friends better help and more assistance that doesn't involve your pocket or overuse of precious energy and free time you have left? What if you could actually know that you're driving your soul and your life/life-force in ways that will definitely be of benefit later on? What if you no longer had to drag karma along with you? Or if – for the first time in your life – you could feel that you are whole and you belong?

What if you missed this shift completely – just like me? OR if you had to die – to then believe it – just like me? But what if – unlike me – you could do nothing more about it? How would you feel?

CHAPTER 32

A whole lifetime isn't long enough to do all you would like to, but the most pressing questions are – will you wake up? Will you make a difference? Will you too help bring in changes on life's higher levels, not to disrupt and turn everything you know, do, love and have accomplished on its head, but from the place and unique standing that you are in now? Can you rise to the occasion, to see things better with more clarity and focus?

(I am I). There is real purpose running through the life you have lived so far that lies deeper than appearances on the surface. Sometimes you cannot see the bigger picture or what's driving

circumstances behind the scenes that unfold or play out.

Sometimes what you go through appears to be more for other people, but in life there are few victims; mostly what occurs will benefit you too on higher levels. Soul contracts cover more than instant needs. Before birth, you wanted to end old and current karma but wanted also to make a difference to help life and those around you that you cared for. Someone, somewhere, must take a lead role in these changes. Sometimes that baton falls to you, for nothing is ever wasted on soul level.

The battle between good and bad, light and dark works itself out within real time. Daily these things surface through all that humans link into and do. The key lies in personal choices, actions, thoughts, decisions and more... You alone will one day answer for what you do and what you missed, what you changed and overcame, what you walked away from, how you too led others or how your actions and connection produced changes then in them.

To be protected is integral to your own security. Life continues always on many *unseen levels, not always nice and pleasant. You will not come to immediate harm – but the changes can be subtle. Over time, they're detrimental to vitality, health and outlook. Why would you not prefer life's better options?*

Believe you are alone – living in a hostile world – and you will be, because you've disconnected from the help that's waiting to assist and to protect, to guide and to uplift you in times of turmoil, stress and change... Believe in what you're learning here and life can assist you in more personal, productive measures, so you can then rest assured that you're working with life correctly, within its realm of creativity, speaking its own evolving multilingual language.

None of life's negatives were ever meant to harm you, but only to unblock, strengthen and heal – to help you to shift blockages and wake up strengths. It's mainly through times like these that true growth can occur – because in times of peace why would you or any other be moved to change things? Why would you try to fix what doesn't show itself as broken? Yet without the need for growth, how would what's old and stale then release?

Every soul has equal chance to overcome birth limitations – but not all will. That's down to personal choice, to personal drive, commitments, to the calling within oneself to do better, to be more, to advance. Every effort made from this soul level will be met with live conditions best to aid its cause and purpose. Each thing overcome takes you onwards towards the next phase of your quest. (I am I).

By waking up while still alive physically, you'll have the chance to re-adjust different aspects of your behaviour and character that you feel important: like what you do, how you think, react, how you want your life to be, what you want most to complete and take with you ongoing, how you link to others and what you expect, what you want to clear away or leave behind....

Many are embarrassed when they review the life they've had – in terms of what they missed, more than what they did, had or produced. It's easy to look back and to believe you've done your best, but often that's more in terms of where priorities were at that moment. When you up your current understanding and then look from other levels, you'll see yourself – not just in terms of you against the world – but more from the part you could have played if you had just seen your connection with fresh open eyes, with better understanding of the charmed position you were in – to make a difference in other ways once your own needs had been met beyond sufficiently.

I myself was now ready to move forward from this mid-place here in Heaven. Because most of us will continue working to help ourselves while helping others, I'd elected that I would teach those who were like the old me – teach what I was learning now, to help them make better sense of their life and what they had been through. I understood this learning didn't only come from one life, but from many lives that I'd lived and been through.

I should have really woken up while still physical. All the signs had been there for a long time. This would have helped me to move forward further over here. But this book will serve that purpose for me now instead. I have my wife to thank for that, that she continued on with her own growth despite the many obstacles I gave without fully understanding why I felt that way. The force was strong...

Life here is lovely. It's like all you hope and wish for coming true – but even better. But it isn't all it could have been had I been able to move forward a bit further. The place that I have reached is just for now. Another stepping stone. Because of writing this book, my physical journey is not over. I can still add to my vibration by what it will accomplish – that's why I said I am lucky.

What you'll achieve on Earth will help you overall, not only there but here, when you get here. Most people have simply hit their own ceiling on development. It's time to punch that through, to understand yourself and why you chose your life and present pathway, to know your strengths and weaknesses and to move forward in directions of birthright, that you deserve or know will bring you growth, to make you happy.

Everything will be OK – just as long as you try your best. Know now you are loved, that you are needed, unique and very special. To stay asleep and live in ignorance is not an option. Life itself is waking up. It's shaking you to wake up along with it, to see what the world's producing and how you too can add more flavour to it – to then make better choices to help change that.

No one will be left behind here. If you're not a pioneer at the forefront of this process, then you still will be affected, but instead you'll bump along, even be dragged along as you'll wonder what is going on – the hard way. Why would you do that to yourself? Why would you choose the hard way because you dare not, don't believe or can't be bothered? Everything will be alright, but you also have to help it while you're part of changing conditions, during the time you are here. It's the whole reason behind why you birthed this time – to be a live part in this process. It's not random good or bad luck that you are here, but personal choice.

Take a look around you – at how far you've come. Notice how you are quite different to many people that you know. Ask yourself why? Ask your higher self why you are not happy – despite all you've done and how you try. Ask what you are here to do or to learn or to put next into place. Learn what makes you happy and feel whole, inspired and connected. What do you still dream of – understand the reasons why. Don't think you're just responsible for your own life and chosen close circles, for life's own ripples and your ability to affect them doesn't stop there. Everything is connected and that means that you are too – with the whole thriving living entity called this planet.

For now, at this moment, there is no need to know too much more of Heaven. You'll find this out for yourself when the time is right for you. Remember that it's huge. Bigger than the Earth, more diverse, more levels, more ways of living life; even more than simple words or imagination can explain or grasp within the limitations of just present language.

Everyone will come in to the level/type of life/ existence they have gained or created through progress. Either you'll progress when you get here or you still won't be able to. No one wants to regress, but some don't have the option if they've lived a life where darkness ruled their choices. If you can't progress, you may elect to come back, to relive, gather and choose from other options to gain growth. But realise that you'll have the same problems again or maybe worse, to shake you up, to wake you up, until the time you realise there is more.

Most people still believe their current story is their lot, their whole life accomplishment, goal or personal payback, unaware that more is waiting to flood in.

If you've looked under every rock and stone and have tried all that you know, if all you've done and have allotted have not produced your *Happy Ever After*, then something more is being missed. Lift your own perspective. Listen, levitate higher, hear what's being said in movies, songs, conversations, conditions and opportunities opening up around you and the wider world. Become aware...

Even this little book is just a stepping stone, a guiding light to more...

SIMON...

A MESSAGE FROM
THE AUTHORS

It took millions of years for Earth to form, but right at the start, *all that existed* did not yet know itself or what was.

> *(I am I). I could not express what had been created because there was no form of educated, conscious, intelligent thought on the planet. No form of language. No way to measure or know. What was there was good, healthy and growing, but there was no knowledge, no way to understand the meaning of anything until humanity was born to experience, to feel, think and to live, to be, know and evolve as all physical*

life growing was offered. But life had to continue beyond that – for Me to know all that had been created would work as it should. I made people to be My eyes, My taste buds, My hearing and touch, to replicate Myself – to complement this live work in progress and to continue what had been begun.

I made humanity in my image as creator. People had to think for themselves because then they could also create. Humanity had to live unencumbered upon the planet that sustains all of life, so I too could fully experience.

I now need humanity to help Me consciously, to stabilise and sustain what has been put into place or produced since time first began. Yes, this world would operate, still continue if people were not here, sure enough, but present time is in a state of imbalance. I need conscious intent and interaction to correct this on My behalf.

Because people have free will and choice, anything that I would do alone would countermand what that freedom stands for. This decision belongs to humanity... Each person must decide for themselves what they wants to do, but the key points are these – that each has been here before, is living here now and most likely will return here again – not out of pressure or malice, but out of love, out of free will and choice. Each will come again at some point in the future to experience what they too created with like-minded others. (I am I).

Good and bad are equal parts of the same whole. Without one, the other could not be known, either by mankind or by God/the universal consciousness/ creation itself. Without comparisons, life would be vanilla. (Remember that the term/label 'God' is only a name, a reference point, like the names we ourselves have been given to be identified/known.)

For us to fully engage and to experience life, we had to be conscious, intelligent, contributing, physical beings. We had to have the attributes of God, to be able to think for ourselves alone, to have the freedom of individual sight, touch, smell, hearing and taste. We had to become explorers from our own moment of birth, and so that is why we're born helpless, like a blank open page awaiting input or a virgin computer without program or aim. All functions are present and possible – we just needed to learn personally of their existence and how then to master and use them.

Humans are born explorers of life. What each person makes of their lifetime is totally their own affair, from beginning to end. Yes, at the start each is at the mercy of their surroundings, but thereafter, once they learn to exercise free will, they adapt – to then do as they please. This is the only way a true exploration can achieve its results – unique, individual results.

Just like a true explorer, a child must have guidelines for understanding, good conduct and safety, but thereafter each will do whatever feels good and works well for themselves going forward.

Adults are little different. They also have guidelines to follow, but each has free will and the discrimination to choose whether those guidelines are correct, valid and useful or not. They can push boundaries at any time and redraw and refine them at others. Just as a child looks to their parents and peers for guidance, so an adult should look within, at their own wealth of knowledge, insight and intuition collected through years – even lifetimes. Each has their own uniquely crafted buttons and triggers designed to serve and to lead them along their own path of discovery.

We all express potential in different ways, meaning that how we live life, each relationship, journey chosen, and expressive creative style will differ depending on what's needed or desired by will or mindset. On the surface we may display what's accepted or expected, but inside another dialogue chatters on and it's this that is responsible for what we think, do, say, express, become...

No one wants to live a harder life than necessary. We each are very different yet very much the same in needs and outlook. Regardless of race or gender, age, intellect, education, wealth or social standing, although we've done our best, we've also made mistakes, even whoppers, but how we overcame them and went forward set the precedent to underpin what happened next.

Yet how often do we stop to re-assess, to over-write, explore and to update the route we are travelling – born from where we've been, from what we've seen and learned to realign, to check the truth, validity, necessity of beliefs still carried and their relevance to what we're doing and where we're heading? Organically life evolves, technology forever updates, but to all intents and purposes, do we?

> *(I am I). Each person gets many chances to reshape, restart and re-assess, if not from baseline scratch, then from a place they have now reached within the storyline they're living and what's been chosen. (I am I).*

Like many people of middle age, I had gone through many challenges and personal changes. Not all were good and nice, not all went in my favour or were chosen at the time first-hand directly. Although I had enjoyed free will, I was completely unaware of unseen forces that govern the type of life we will choose, directions we then travel and will live. I believed myself in full control, but now in hindsight, it seems I wasn't – for emotions, thoughts and feelings present would tell me otherwise. Having weathered all I had, life again would come up short of goals and expectations. Something was always missing, something I couldn't name, explain or pin-point, much less gain...

> *(I am I). These things are symptoms of inner stirring or soul calling – as your higher self shifts to reawaken because of goal posts reached. But few realise or understand where these feelings come from, where their personal growth is at or that they've simply reached a ceiling of their present level of life and soul development, a time of change. (I am I).*

Every reader will extrapolate what they need to from this plain, straight-talking book to increase their own awareness of what they're living and expressing – to make things better, to gain further understanding, explanation, insight, deeper love, health, bliss and happiness today, to make their life make sense. It's no longer quite enough to wait and see what may occur when this present timespan is over, because the consequences of what happened, of things gained, attained, missed, misused or abused are more far-reaching than we acknowledge or even think about daily, today.

What if, when you passed depending on that outcome, you found it necessary to repeat certain aspects of what you'd been through once again, because you'd somehow missed the actual meaning or valued point of things you had been through? Or what if what had been applied was still not quite enough to propel you forward towards the place or levels you'd want to move in next? Would you be accepting, happy or annoyed that whilst living you hadn't known? Who and what would you be mad at? What if then the best or only option for improvement/change was to re-birth again quickly to do better, before what's left behind and still unfolding becomes ingrained, entrenched through your behaviour or lack of action, unchanged by what could have been accomplished had you realised...?

These are not pretend scenarios plucked from a magician's hat, but very real possibilities if our higher purpose, or happenings behind occurrences we could have grown from, changed or altered were somehow missed...

As a son, father, colleague, friend and more, I really thought I'd had life figured out. I tried my utmost to do things well, to leave no task unfinished, large or small, no stone unturned. But in the end, was I happy? Did I manage to find the balance, truth, contentment, love and purpose I desired or felt I deserved or had intended from these actions? And what defined me really – external tasks displayed or the relentless inner dialogue that few or sometimes no one witnessed, that drove my character and fuelled behaviour which then became me?

If life really doesn't continue beyond the point of death, then how we had just lived and spent a lifetime would not matter. All would then be over and we'd be none the wiser beyond that happening.

But that's not the case. Many good, intelligent, hard-working people are feeling let down whilst still here, disillusioned by life, society and even by friends and family, despite sharing obvious loving actions and achievements. They somehow live a half-life, locked inside a storyline they believe and add to through behaviour and conditioning, even when – from an outside view – their life looks happy, shiny and bigger, seeing life more as though through a filter than as the reality of what's really happening. With hand on heart, many do the best they can to battle on or to tread through time and life as though treading on water. But when life is finally over on body level, as it will be at some stage for one and all, it's too late to then admit, to realise or decide that you want to make some changes, large or subtle.

If we all completely knew for certain that life continues and the consequences then attached to that bold statement, we'd value and take more care of time spent here. We'd care better for ourselves, for our communities and the wider planet; we'd be more careful in our actions, with resources and with how we use our life force. But more importantly, we'd understand exactly what we're part of and why we're here, that what we go through is not for nothing, that it shapes and makes the real true us, that we attract what next comes up and we'd leave a better wake behind us after passing. And because we had prepared, we'd be more equipped to face the music from our actions.

We do not die – we go on living! Body itself is only temporary. When it falls away – what is then left? There's only change, transition, transformation and soul growth! Aside from the grief of family, friends and relatives when you pass, it's a shock to find that you're still present when your body is clearly not. Again the repercussions of this knowledge are enormous…

What if this information is completely new to you? Can you say you're sure there is no need to research further? How can you say you don't believe it – if you've never looked into it more deeply to decide, examine, check? Not in terms of religion, creed and dogma, but in terms of your attachment to life itself – to know the real you? What holds you back?

What are you so afraid you might find out? What if all is true? What would that mean to you? Aren't you glad you are still here to be able now to check, to then tweak and make some changes you'll find appropriate? No matter when, how, where or for how long, would it not be better to embrace even the possibility while still present here in physical life rather than to pass and so find out that more exists – but you had missed it?

To have travelled through a lifetime but not have moved further forward or to have grown at all would be a shame. Isn't it better, safer to *know* you're on the right track, than to find out later there was more, that life and opportunities contained much higher meanings to help you grow, reshape and progress?

> *(I am I). No one is immune from cause and effect, from karma, from seen/unseen laws of attraction and the results of personal choices, actions and creations. You use free will and free choice without charge. What you give your life force to, and what you then freely do, also have no charge. Do you ever stop to question why, when in an all-pervading, powerful universe such as this, you can freely make life-changing choices over ME – that overrule ME?*

Through the ages, sages and wise people tried their best to explain and speak out honestly and openly about life's continuity. But educated, intellectual minds couldn't grasp it because it's simple – for some minds much too simple to believe. That's why a child's mind is much better. It's open, less assuming, less polluted, unbiased, unconditioned, until it's then told what to think and what to say, what to believe, expect and how to do it and to behave... (I am I).

This book is a powerful read, a game changer. Every one alive right now will at some point die in some personal manner. How and when this will occur there is no need to know, but what we haven't yet seemed to grasp is that life itself can't and doesn't stop for any person. It continues. We continue. We continue on without the density or form of our current body, a body that until that point was reached had kept us physical. We continue on with every other aspect that defined our individual self still intact – memory, character, past experience, conscious identity, awareness, conscience and soul blueprint...

Life does not end. It cannot end. It can't be stamped out, snuffed out or destroyed – but body can. Were we simply skin and bone and here just for the section of time lived between our birth and death, how would we evolve? Instead we'd swiftly run out of reasons to be present. We'd destroy ourselves and this planet too in a single lifetime spent. Yet that's not the case. Death is the illusion, an imposter. Yes, when body is old or damaged you will cease to be as you are now, but in truth you'll reach a new point of transition, you'll be still alive; you'll still think, feel, know and love exactly as you do at this moment – but even more so, because what holds you back today in terms of body's 'isms' will not exist.

Don't wait until it's too late to realise where you are going, not too late to experience life, but too late to put it to good use or to know your true self and your function…

During the course of living life, it's easy to become and even stay blocked. It may take time and effort to correct this within the self, because as time passes by it's generally easier to compound a problem, than to acknowledge and address it.

A Perfect World...

Once upon a time there lived a man. He was a simple man both in needs and desires. Then one day he found a magic lamp. He rubbed the lamp and a genie appeared.

"I can grant to you your heart's desire," the genie said, "but only on the condition that it will bring you happiness."

The man thought for a while. He considered all the options that were available to him – riches, travel, gems, women, friends and neighbours, fast cars, corporate business, holidays, jet planes, boats, fame, etc, etc. He looked at the possibility of owning or experiencing those things. He searched his mind for the outcome and the pleasure those things would surely offer him. He thought of the women... He thought of the popularity... He thought and thought about all it would bring and mean. At last he had made up his mind.

"I wish for every man to be at peace with his life. I wish for heartache and sorrow, illness and fatigue to be things of the past. I wish for each person to attain their own personal goals and I wish for them to be content with their choice. I wish for world hunger, illness and deprivation to be no more. I wish for each person to get all that they need to survive. But most of all I wish for love. I wish for each and every person to have the deepest love they desire."

The genie laughed. "But these things are yours already. All you ask is already in place."

"How so?" said the man. "I look about me and see only famine and war. Some people kill and others are sad. Most never achieve their dream of success or their pot of gemstones or gold. They argue to get love and the respect they deserve, so do their children and friends. Famine is rife in half of the world, while the rest has more than its share... How can you say my wishes are already in place?"

The genie smiled. He looked the man in the eye for a while. Then he looked to the right and destruction was there, desire and heartache too. So were man's hopes and dreams, achievements and abilities. He looked to the left and it was the same. All was in place. But mankind still had a long way to go in terms of finding true happiness.

"I can do no more to fulfil your request," the genie said. "All is in its proper place. It is up to mankind to fill in the blanks for a wonderful love-filled future."

The man was put out. "But my wishes – where are they?"

The genie just shook his head sadly.

"I have given you the Earth, the sky and free love – a life that is full to the brim. I can do no more. The rest is up to you. If you cannot love one another, the rest will not matter. No riches and dreams will fulfil you. The love that you search for is with you from now till the end."

He was gone in a flash – no more than that.

The man just stood there a while.

The genie was God, who had come to give help to mankind. The rest has still not been written...

(This story excerpt was taken from – AND SO IT BEGINS...
Visit www.stephaniejking.com for further details...)

We each hold the key to our own future.

The past has been and is gone. We live in the present, a product of today. The future will be fine, because the present where we live is written and rewritten day by day. It's a product of love, of peace, of contentment, commitment, hard work and hope – hope that the future will be bright. And it will be, as long as we each play our part. And as we each do come back to live here again, it matters very much what we make of the life we are in.

Over the strands of time we have done many things to make life comfortable for ourselves and for others, and in this respect we keep going, we enjoy the comfort of past inventions, but what do we do in the future? When material life gets as good as it can get, what will we put our efforts into? Will we just want more of the same? Once survival and comfort have been achieved, what more should we do? What more should we plough time and effort into?

We come into this world with nothing but the life we are given. When we leave, we take that life force back with us to the place where we all belong and graduate to, but what of all the wealth and possessions we have accumulated during that life? What of all the good intentions we had and the things we intended to do with them?

What matters more than any possession is the way we have just lived our life – the happiness and the love we shared, the good things that have resulted from the fact that we have been here, the legacy of courage, strength, truth, love and knowledge that we have left behind – even in the smallest seed which can grow and make a difference. That is what we each take forward with us – as life's offering...

What you leave behind equates to input, energy. When you reassess, you will have been an asset or a drain. What you did as free will, choice and action added more to what occurred. Will the end result be what you thought it would be, what you wanted or even wished for?

Be glad you are still here to look again.

Simon and Stephanie

FURTHER INSPIRATIONAL CONVERSATIONS

The purpose of this book is to help you understand life continues.

Very real consequences follow on from the actions and choices we make here.

You and your life are important – not only for the reasons you expect.

Death is a transition not an end.

Body is a cloak, a shell, an external casing – that's all. It's not who you are but the mechanism that transports and supports you through this present passage of time.

Many life experiences have been travelled through to increase your vibrancy and awareness.

Everything you are and have been is not all you will grow to become.

No one knows you like you know yourself but you still are finetuning and upgrading.

Every atom of your being links in to something much bigger.

Soul is eternal. Eternal means you existed before and still will once this lifetime is over.

What you do with your life force, what you make of time spent here, will matter greatly to you once this present experience is over.

Everyone will go through their own unique issues to help them to birth what only they can to make changes, to bring in something better born from it.

Reality is based on perception. This will differ according to mindset, understanding, intent and experience gained.

Every person has a purpose, a unique reason to be here right now.

Birth limitations were chosen for reasons beyond the apparent – to be transcended as appropriate.

Everything will be overcome.

Know that you are enough and go forward with that knowledge and mindset.

Time is not what you think it to be – it is more.

You are more than your understanding to this point.

You are evolving; awakening is part of this process.

Your soul knows what you are, what you need and how to get there.

Life will support you when you express, engage and communicate life directives productively and clearly in tune with what is now required.

Every person must choose what will universally happen next for them.

Everyone here is still growing.

Images you hold in your thoughts and beliefs attract to you even more of the same.

For life to unfold in the way you most want – change your thinking and end perspective.

Find what is hidden, often out of view, beneath or behind present dramas.

Begin to know yourself better, not from what is seen or what you show, but from the unconscious programme that drives/propels you.

Push beyond what you'd usually expect.

Non-action, open mind and wonder are powerful game changers.

What if you missed what you came to life for?

Each unimportant day is a gift.

Will you begin to recognise the route you've travelled through life and then explore why?

What we do to each other we do to ourselves, because we'll carry it forward through karma...

Not all you've gone through was necessary.

Lay down your burdens – let life assist with solutions.

Your aura is your protection. Don't trash it through actions unthinking – yet wilfully chosen.

Become aware of patterns you're stuck in.

Know that you alone are in charge of your life force.

Step out of old out of date programmes that harm or hold you back.

When you hurt others by will, action or word, you become responsible for what next unfolds.

Very little is as it would seem.

You are here on a journey of exploration, discovery and awakening.

What you do in this life determines what will happen in the next – whether you're in body or not.

What would you feel like if you completely overlooked something huge, something so fundamental to your personal existence that you'd have to come back here again?

Not everyone thinks like you do. Begin to notice what drives you and why.

Every moment and thought has potential.

Don't get sad or mad. Do better. Be the example that all can see, connect to and follow.

Become aware of your footprint. What will you leave in your wake?

Open your eyes and your mind.

Release your negative thinking or you'll add more to what you don't really want.

Step away from drama and hype.

Find the highest truth, the real bottom line, and move forward.

Know that nothing can ever be hidden. All converts back to energy and karma. Do only what you're happy to own.

Each lifetime you live is yet one more chance to do better.

Everything you add to – you will be responsible for.

Life is changing. Learn and grow with it.

Don't measure your worth by what you have been and done so far. You've hit a ceiling, a new wave/level of growth – evolution is flowing in.

Tomorrow does not always come. Seize today.

You are part of creation. What you think and believe you stick onto life as live labels. At some point you'll have these to own up to.

What are you giving to life?

What would your life story say personally about you to God?

It's never too late to stand still, to readjust and take stock.

It's important to wake up to higher truths whilst still in this life.

Don't let anyone tell you how to be.

Most things that stand in your way come from fear born of others or from you.

Create your happiness now. Come back to inner balance and peace.

Be responsible for your current actions.

Be the difference you hope for or seek.

Death is your body falling away from your soul. Be careful of what you'll take along with you.

Knowing that life does continue makes the time you live here more precious.

Learn why you've lived all you have.

Release what you don't really need – to feel lighter, brighter, more buoyant.

Everything will work out just right – but you must wake up to what you're attracting/creating.

Where you are is where you should be for the next stage of your life to kick in.

Nothing is lost, missed or broken; you've just reached a point that needs change.

First you must see a good picture of life, to attract what you next want to appear.

Those you have loved and thought you had lost are still close. They know what you think and you feel. Give them your love not your sadness or anger. Let them enjoy your success as you grow.

Habits and bad patterns must be recognised, worked through, understood and released while you're here.

Only keep going what you want to repeat or continue.

You have free will and free choice, the ability to create and to move in any direction. Why would you limit yourself? Why would you not recognise that's a gift?

What you are you offer to life as your payback for having been here.

It's easy to get caught in the crossfire or confusion of others. Stand still; release what's not needed or relevant. Do nothing to add more yourself.

Get out of the way of your clamouring thoughts.

Say 'STOP' and let peace come back in.

What do you need from life next? Take small sure steps to let this unfold.

Don't push. Pull back. Wait for the right time and move with it.

Don't harm or hurt. To do so will instead harm yourself as like attracts more like and karma.

Don't waste your life or your life force. Make memories, travel, explore, love, learn and grow; you can't have this moment again.

Be open to possibilities that are good as you are – there's still more to be/understand…

Always look beyond what's apparent.

You are strong; you are wise; you can work out the truth for yourself.

What you stand for and become is the vibration you then gain as payback. In the next level as soul without body, this will determine completely where you'll live and what life will be like.

When you feel you are broken or lost – that's when new growth can begin.

To help, heal or strengthen yourself and your aura...

- Remember to visualise yourself in a bubble of pure brilliant white light. To do so will serve to protect you.

- Imagine electric blue energy around you for healing.

- Red is deep love, strength and abundance. Visualise yourself walking in it – to ground and connect deeply with life.

- Yellow or gold is more willpower, energy... Imagine bright rays of the sun surrounding and holding you now.

- Green is new growth, protection and planet awareness. Embrace the shimmers of emerald, immerse yourself in them right now...

- Orange – not liked by all – is important. You need it for self-love and personal acceptance, for vitality, sexuality and for your internal organs to work well...

- Light blue – sky blue, will aid you in terms of verbalising true communication. Speak only the truth based in fact and love, without malice or deliberate outcome/effect. Remain innocent. Least said soonest mended. Move forward.

- Violet – the colour created and worn through time by royalty – is your GOD connection. The more you connect – the more it can be seen before you with your eyes closed. Envelope yourself completely in it now.

- Hand everything back out to the universe – so growth, insight, higher knowledge can appear...

- Draw in pure white light through your body, from the top of your head, flowing out through your feet. Allow a cloak of protection, a cloak of pure white light to surround you.

- Life made you perfect. Allow yourself to honour that now.

- Like the phoenix or the hybrid – rise up to embrace your true self.

- Stand in the light, let your true self be seen – an example that others can follow.

- If what you intend harms another, don't do it. Stop – come back to innocence and base. Ask for higher insight, love, truth, compassion, solutions and balance instead.

- Positive and negative are two opposite ends of the same spectrum. You alone choose your alignment.

- Be the love and the happiness you seek – for it to then keep flooding back...

- Remember that the body itself is only temporary. Instead there's only change, transition, transformation and soul growth! When the body falls away – what then is left?

- What if a whole lifetime spent here is not quite enough to take you forward in directions you'll then choose? What will you do? Who will you want to blame and why?

- Everyone dies – but not all are pleased with their life results.

- How you overcome life and challenges really matters.

- Before you leave this life, before your time is done, ensure you're really happy with your achievements.

- We're just returning to life's own language long forgotten...

ALSO BY STEPHANIE J. KING

Stephanie's works have been specifically channelled to help you work through karma and what's occurring now – love, work, family, home – to highlight what lies hidden, to fine tune your highest attributes, strengths and gifts, and to help you to regain, to remember what has been lost.

Internationally known and respected – Stephanie J. King – Soulpreneur™ – has worked directly with the (I am I) consciousness and the higher Spiritual / Celestial realms for many decades – to re-awaken the soul; to channel guidance, inspiration, enlightenment, encouragement, self-empowerment and healing that's both powerful and applicable to all…

And So It Begins

You have more power over life than you realise

This is the first book written in a series destined to rebuild the hopes and happiness of man, who has thought himself unworthy and abandoned for far too long. Man is connected to the true source of life, to the source of the planet itself. He has never been anything other.

Man was born to live the life that is here now. This is his heritage, not his punishment. Man was meant to be happy, living his choices, not downtrodden and depressed. *And So It Begins* mirrors aspects of character that rarely get considered. It helps unburden clutter, blindly passed down through generations, to gently reseat the deepest foundations. The time that each person has left and how he chooses to use it is the key to his future, and his future begins here –physically and spiritually 'now'. This is the legacy.

> *(I am I) How many people recognise my hand in life? How many understand that I know their every thought, wish and movement? How many realise I am not the vengeful ruling force they think me to be? How many wish for love and recognition but realise it is already within – just waiting to be unlocked and fully lived? (I am I)*

And So It Begins will take you by the hand and lead you forward in a way that is safe and realistic to be beneficial from the very first time that you use it. Every soul alive is born with a life agenda – chosen by him and higher beings – for his own soul's improvement. Each is on a journey of awakening and discovery. Each is placed in life where they can best achieve what needs to be accomplished and experienced.

Every soul, therefore every life, links directly to Earth, to Source, to the Universal Consciousness itself. *And So It Begins* opens windows and doors to new insights and understanding that you may not have realised existed. Like an oracle/truth-mirror/real-time life guide, it will quickly highlight your soul purpose and life agenda. You'll know exactly who you are, what you're part of, what's going on with others and life around you, what you're able to achieve and contribute, where and why things get stuck as well as ways you can effortlessly change this. You'll view differently past and present; your karma, talents, gifts and strengths, how others push your buttons and why you react – to stop repeating what you no longer need.

From teenager to elderly this book is already helping thousands to reassess what they've known, to rekindle dreams and goals, to turn life around and be happy. It highlights the negativities playing out in the present – to give you more choice and actually spins things around for the better. Read it as a book or dip into its pages (perfect for busy lifestyles), you'll actually feel yourself interacting with higher levels, with Source, with your own Spirit Guardian/Angel/Guide and with life – as if in direct conversation with a personal friend on a soul to soul level.

Empowered and completely in tune with where you are, you'll breeze through all aspects of life/ love/ work/family/home and move forward with ease, clearing clutter and blockages accumulated through generations and the years that you've personally been here – but make no mistake – this is not like any other book you have previously read for self-development. *And So It Begins* will make a difference in your life and outlook right from the start. You'll feel healthier and happier with renewed energy and confidence, positivity, focus and life zest. This book is perfect for the already developed mind as well as for the beginner.

Helping you to also help others, you'll become a light worker – for what you give out will always come back. In this manner you'll help life heal itself.

> *(I am I) The life force that is yours is unique. No one else can fill your shoes. No one else has had your same life experience. I need you to come back consciously to truths that wait here for you – to help ease your life 'now' and help you grow. (I am I)*

And So It Begins can be used many times daily for up to the minute guidance that's completely in tune with what's happening around and about you, and as you receive this information – life will immediately respond in accordance. The help you need is here – the rest is up to you.

Life is Calling

How to Manifest Your Life Plan

Are you aware that you're living a live real-time soul journey and that your limited time span here contains targets, purpose and goals? That you have talents, strengths and tasks to accomplish and contribute? That you were born with a pre-chosen life agenda of your own? That you've lived on earth before? That you create your own reality and that daily life needs and takes instructions straight from you? Do you know you connect to earth's own creative, thinking mind and that everything about you interacts?

Each day is a new day. It is another chance to create, to make a difference, to redraw and redefine who you are and what you do. How you live, interact and connect with daily life means everything – for all achievements you'll take with you, back to the realms of Spirit – as your contribution and offering to life, to physicality and to time.

Written like a deck of cards (with over 380 entries) but in an easy to manage book form, *Life is Calling* was channelled by Spirit as a direct 'soul to soul' interchange. It's a link to advice for you from your own Guardian/Angel/Guide in a down to earth way that completely connects and relates to where you are. It will mirror everything as it highlights information that will prove relevant from the very first time that you use it.

Nothing happens by chance. You know everything about yourself, your thoughts, situations, history and events. You know what you believe in. Each time you pick it up *Life is Calling* will correspond to now and be precise in the guidance, words and knowledge being given. It will completely turn around, balance and correct many things that you both consciously and subconsciously do – so you can choose and re-choose as you go along, depending on what's playing out.

Life is Calling will help you manifest your own life plan step by step – and before long you will know exactly what that is and where you're heading... Labelled a phenomenon, this incredible interactive book will take you by the hand and deliver specific, tailored guidance at the precise time and place you need it most. It can be surprising to realise how much you matter and that someone, something, somewhere, knows you better than you even know yourself, better than your own mother, loved ones, family and friends do – for your Guardian has always been with you – never judging, just helping and silently waiting for you to notice. Perfect for busy lifestyles, this powerful guide book will help you to change much for the better, as you access higher truths and information that are with you.

Link and work directly with life's own creative forces. Interact with Source – as if being taken by the hand – so pure data, insights, inspiration, hunches and extrasensory information can filter through. Increase performance, optimise results, and reach targets and personal short and long term life goals easily, without an increase in effort from you – through renewed understanding and insight. Love, work, family and home – all results will be immediate and immense. This book has the potential to enhance the rest of your life – for the rest of the time frame that you live here.

Life Is Calling Concise Pocket/Handbag Version

Due to popular demand *Life is Calling* is also now available in an abridged pocket/ handbag size version. Many people love our book so much that nearly 200 entries 'specifically chosen by spirit' form this book – in a small easy to travel fashion size to see you through the day at random times.

Divine Guidance

The answers you need to make miracles

We physically live the miracle of life on this living, breathing, thriving planet every day. We have free choice and free will. We have the ability to love and grow; to move in any direction and to climb the highest heights that we can dare. Yet how often are we free to feel happy?

Divine Guidance is designed to work with you in the unfolding drama of your life story – in all ways unique and connected to you. It links to higher conscious mind through your own intelligence, through your energetic life force and higher self, linking with and through your Guardian straight to Source/God/Earth/the Universal Source of Life that links to all. This book will take you by the hand to steer you through whatever is occurring to lead you forward, supporting, advising, to help you achieve the highest outcome available at any moment.

Miracles are a natural part of daily life – we just don't notice. According to your wants and needs life is trying to unfold in your best interest. But circumstances, thoughts, doubts, fears, emotions and many more things get in the way. Not all you hear, see, feel or know is beneficial...

What possibilities would await if you could navigate the life you live more effectively, staying one step ahead of others and of change? What if you always had a solution for the many challenges you face – to ease your journey? Do you want the best from what love, family, friendship, home, work and finance have to offer?

Life is not always as it seems. Underlying issues, perception cause and effect, karma, intention and soul purpose simultaneously play out together on levels unseen. For the seemingly miraculous to happen, for life to function properly, all aspects and all facets must work in sync – including us.

Life is not against you – it's working with you, providing daily what you ask for and what you need – though you may not realise... This is always the driving factor that drives life.

Deep within your psyche, within your own survival system, a higher sense of 'being' is creeping forward – you're part of something major going on – it's why you're here... Your own soul is ascending, a new world order is birthing through, you are evolving. Divine Guidance is written to help you recognise where you are within your journey and life agenda – so you can harness your personal power and regain control – regardless of what's unfolding in your now. Every time you use this book you'll get precisely what you need – without exception.

Divine Guidance has the power to make a difference in your life; are you ready to use it...

Believe & Achieve

The answers to teen success (especially great for adults too)

You are a living breathing work of art in a state of constant progress. You're creating and expressing even now as you read these words...

Nothing about you is haphazard. You choose your presentation, clothes, hair and makeup, the food you eat, music preferences, what you laugh and cry at, the books you read, TV programmes, films, hobbies and games you play, the type of friends you chill and mix with, how you spend your free time, conversation, sense of humour and more besides.

This book contains all you need to discover, to realise and understand your life's quest. But are you brave enough to give it a try?

Being a teen is the most important part of your development so far, yet it's often when you feel least acknowledged and understood. What would you like to change? What would it take for you to feel truly happy?

You have enormous potential; you can go anywhere and do all you wish... Love, security, happiness, abundance and success can be yours – much easier and faster than you think. In fact nothing need ever hold you back. But do you even know you are powerful – not powerless – and that life itself is willing you on?

You are part of the generation that will take life forward. Yours is the new wave of creativity and intellect. You see first-hand the world you'll inherit and you feel strongly about much that you deal with. Nothing is impossible. All options are open for you to explore and enjoy. This book will help you to finally BELIEVE in all you are and ACHIEVE all you are capable of and all you were born to be...

Access Your Happiness NOW
TRANSFORMATIONAL HOME WORKSHOP
– delivered via email in bite size segments every 3rd day for 14 days (plus two extra bonus gifts).

Private – Easy – Powerful sessions – with a short five minute film to watch and a couple of pages to read and then process. In six weeks or less you'll see and feel a new you emerge – completely in-tune with your power; working and understanding life better; freed from baggage and hang ups of the past...

This powerful, inspirational, informational – yet incredibly easy set of video coaching sessions, mediations and exercises – is designed to free you from the confines of the past, lifting the lid on what unconsciously drives you to bring long lasting love to the fore and get life again working in tune with your needs; revealing a stronger, happier, healthier, more vibrant and confident you...

Know what holds you back; what and how you attract life; what has become your replacement for love... Know what you need to feel loved and how you too love – friends, lovers, loved ones or self (sometimes the hardest love ever achieved)...

Begin to see clearly what threads through your life drive, overshadow, control you... We'll speak about Karma, Reincarnation, Ego, Soul Agenda, Baggage and Patterns held onto or carried onto, Self Healing, Family Tree/Life Healing, Abundance, Lack, Love and the laws of the Cause, Effect and Attraction.

Nothing will change until you start to change it – and this workshop shows you easily how!

Love, Health, Success and Happiness are far easier to achieve than you think...

Available now from www.stephaniejking.com

Stepping Stones to Change your Life – An easy but powerful HOME WORKSHOP – especially for the corporate mind...

For decades everyone has been working this huge but heavy, backbone of society - corporate machine, in ways that in the past always worked. But life's not the same any more. It's changing. It doesn't respond to what two plus two should actually make. It needs fresh ideas; a completely new approach to problems at home and at work that you too daily face.

Ideas are waiting inside of you. They always have been. This workshop will help you get them out and actuate the intelligent thinker, the unique, resourceful side of yourself that's been waiting to help you be more than you even dared to dream.

Stepping Stones to Change your Life was created to support my brand new video-coaching home workshop – perfect for busy lives and lifestyles – to get you and your life kick started to receive better things…

Every inspiration, idea, invention or light bulb moment stems from somewhere, from a place not only inside of yourself but from influences around about you seen or unseen…

This completely new workshop is generated for the more corporate, grounded mindset to help you move beyond repeating the left brain's usual thought form cycles that produce what's always expected, automatically – into a more creative, fly-by-the-seat-of-your-pants, ground breaking inspiration / action approach.

Nothing limits you – more than you yourself.

So NOW let's change this!

'I Am' Meditations

Channelled Directly from Spirit

'I Am' is the first in a series of guided meditations unique in content and approach, allowing you to work directly with Source – to bring in health, balance, harmony, understanding, forgiveness, love, light, peace, growth and extra sensory information – from the highest realms – to aid all. Because your own journey is unique, your needs, questions and inspirations will be also.

Before birth we each devised a real-time soul agenda, an overall life plan, with live tasks to set in motion, to recognise and work through. We have qualities to contribute, to overcome and accomplish, gifts that we alone can hone and harness to feed directly back to life as personal input, as our contribution and thanks for time spent here.

Many things are answered as you reassess your lot – with the aid of personal guides/your guardian/ and with Source. Physically, nothing is completely certain except we birth and die, yet far more occurs on levels unseen than we can ever imagine. The soul journey you are travelling is completely individual and unwritten – so what you will contribute, pay forward, or give back – is yours by personal choice and accomplishment...

(I am I) I will work with you – if you will work with me (I am I).

'I Am' Meditations - II

HIGHER STILL

'I am' Meditations are the perfect solution to inner wisdom, higher guidance, clarity and focus for the busy lives we lead. Information is always available – for the Universe knows what we need and what is lacking – our soul agenda and potential. So it's natural that we're supported as our real-time living story continues to unfold...

'HIGHER STILL' the second in a series of powerful guided mediations, is even stronger in channelled energy, for what was given in live recording will flow to you directly – to bring in health, abundance, balance, harmony, understanding, forgiveness, love, light, peace, growth and extra sensory information – in tune with where you are, from higher realms.

Before birth we each devised a real-time soul agenda, an overall plan that now plays out. What we don't complete in this life will go forward with us to the next as Earthly Baggage, to again become our karma later on.

We have an opportunity to make a difference, to make life work. We are ascending. Life and energy are speeding up to assist us with this process. The time to make adjustments is right NOW.

Stephanie's works have been specifically channelled to help you work through what's occurring NOW – in matters of love, work, family, home – to highlight what lies hidden, to fine tune higher strengths, to help you to remember and re-gain what you have lost...

(I am I) I will work with you – if you will work with Me (I Am I).

In these mediations you'll actually hear Stephanie's speaking voice change as the higher realms speak through her and use her voice... All energies received during live recording – will NOW directly flow to you – as nothing has been altered or removed... They're very powerful...

'I Am' Angelic Messenger Cards

Simple yet intricate and highly responsive, this beautiful set of 44 quality, handcrafted, Angel Cards is ideally suitable for both professional and private use, including for those awakening (first timers), or for those who want to take their current gifts to the new higher levels now birthing through.

Each card depicts its own particular Angel. Each Angel being greatly expressive, will link to what is needed now or to what's driving circumstances and events upcoming. Each carries its own message, truths and affirmation to help, guide and support your life, granting insights and messages from higher realms. As you connect to life, it's only natural that life communications and connects back to complete the link.

This unique set, slightly larger than a standard playing card, is easy to handle and to shuffle. Their high quality finish with beautifully gilded edging makes them easy to clean with no more than a damp cloth when necessary.

Place your cards into a crystal bowl – then juju them around and choose one for instant guidance. The key word on each card gives you simple instant meanings at that moment. For deeper messages view the book that comes along with them in the set, in a beautiful strong box to keep them safe. Additional layouts and ways to use your new cards are included also – to further help you…

These high energy cards connect to the (I am I) frequency, to the Universal Life Force/Source/God energies themselves. Not to be underestimated, they will prove their worth as brilliant – from the first time that you use them, regardless of reason, question or event.

Powerful, insightful and very special – you'll find them perfect.

'I Am I' Angelic Messages Oracle Book...

Based on the original images of the 'I Am' Angelic Messenger Cards, this book give even fuller, deeper meanings to each card that's depicted within its pages. The Oracle Book can be used in conjunction with the cards above or as a stand alone product to grant you what you need at any moment.

Archangels form the basis of this book and connect to the angels of the cards.

Associated crystals are given to every card, with its longer, deeper message and core guidance, to help you heal and resonate at the frequency your energy needs most at that time.

Powerful affirmations adorn every page.

Popular world prayers grace the rear of the 'I Am I' Angelic Messages Oracle Book as powerful mantras within their own right, even if you only use them in part...

Remember the reason you are awakening now... Life needs your support and for you to work with it closer than you have been.

(I am I) As you do - you'll feel My live connection,

My strength, My Protection and My Love – Unconditional. (I am I).

'Believe & Achieve' Meditations

INCREASE INTUITION AND AWARENESS

PERFECT FOR TEENS AND THE INNER CHILD IN ADULTS...

You are part of the generation that will take life forward. Yours is the new wave of creativity and intellect birthing through. You see first-hand the world that you'll inherit and you feel strongly about much you have to deal with. Yet nothing is impossible. All options are open for you to explore, fine tune, reshape, invent and enjoy.

These special, guided meditations were downloaded to precisely help you understand your own power and potential. Very quickly you'll find yourself more focused, relaxed and open to new ideas flowing in, and because you'll stress and anger less, relationships on all levels will feel the benefit. The brilliance of who you are will be apparent for all to see. Life will flow far easier in the directions you most want – and you'll be happy. Intuition and insight will increase.

Stephanie

FOR FURTHER INFORMATION -

TO KEEP ABREAST OF APPEARANCES, NEW RELEASES, MAGAZINE AND BLOG ENTRIES – VISIT:

www.stephaniejking.com

NOTES

NOTES

NOTES

NOTES

NOTES

CPSIA information can be obtained
at www.ICGtesting.com
Printed in the USA
BVHW041158220121
598416BV00008B/417